WESTMAR COLLE

John P. Manning

THE COMMERCE POWER
VERSUS STATES RIGHTS

THE
COMMERCE POWER
VERSUS
STATES RIGHTS

"BACK TO THE CONSTITUTION"

By EDWARD S. CORWIN

*McCormick Professor of Jurisprudence in
Princeton University*

1936 · *PRINCETON*
PRINCETON UNIVERSITY PRESS
LONDON · HUMPHREY MILFORD
OXFORD UNIVERSITY PRESS

PRINTED AT THE PRINCETON UNIVERSITY PRESS
PRINCETON, NEW JERSEY, U.S.A.

ACKNOWLEDGMENT

I acknowledge with appreciation the aid afforded by a grant from the Social Science Research Council in preparing this work for the press.

E. S. C.

PREFACE

"*BACK to the Constitution*" *is the motto of this small volume, and by* "*Constitution*" *is meant the Constitution of George Washington, Alexander Hamilton, James Madison (the Madison of 1787, not of 1798, nor of 1829), and of John Marshall; not the* "*interested sophistications*" *of those later foster fathers of the Constitution, certain distinguished counsel who about 1890 began, with the too frequent aid of a sympathetic Court, to enmesh the powers of the National Government in* "*a network of juridical niceties.*"

In 1789 Congress was deemed to have the same power over commerce among the States as over that with foreign nations, the same right to restrain the one as the other for what it thought to be the good of the country, and a hundred years later judicial interpretation of the Constitution still had not changed on these points. But recent decisions reflect very different doctrine, even while they confine it for the most part to national action touching productive industry, and particularly the employer-employee relationship in such industry. Nor is this sort of inconsistency to be found in the decisions alone. Thus it would be interesting to know how many of those who are at present urging the National Government, in the furtherance of safer betting, to prevent the passage of "*doped*" *racing steeds from one State to another, belong to the American Liberty League. And how many members of that organization would care to have the National Government repeal the laws under which it today cooperates with the States in combating crime, or to lower its tariff walls to the products of foreign "cheap labor"? Yet when, on the other hand, it is suggested that Congress has power to prohibit interstate commerce in goods produced by concerns whose unsocial methods enable them to undersell their competitors in the interstate market, then we are informed that the Federal System and States Rights are in imminent peril!*

"The Constitution of the United States," said Woodrow Wilson, "is not a mere lawyer's document: it is a vehicle of life, and its spirit is always the spirit of the age." Decisions like those setting aside the Railway Retirement Act, the A. A. A., and the Guffey Act, put all such optimistic pronouncements in abeyance for the nonce. Fortunately those decisions were not by a unanimous Court. One indeed was denounced by three of the Court's most learned and most esteemed members as resting on "a tortured construction of the Constitution." That this characterization was a just one, the materials assembled in these pages go far to show. By the same sign they afford ground for belief that the Court will still undo the damage it has done.

For it is always essential in discussing constitutional questions to keep in mind the great fundamental truth conveyed in Mr. Warren's words: "However the Court may interpret the Constitution, it is still the Constitution which is the law and not the decision of the Court" (The Supreme Court in United States History, *III*, *470*).

Also, there is a second, though scarcely secondary, interest attaching to the materials here assembled, besides the light which they throw on the history of the commerce power. For they also afford a cross-section of judicial review as an institution of popular government. The story they tell is one of aggrandizement, which has become especially accelerated in the national field within recent years. In the final result the Court has transferred to itself a generous slice of Congress's discretion in the exercise of the national legislative power.

May 26, 1936   EDWARD S. CORWIN

TABLE OF CONTENTS

CHAPTER ONE

INTRODUCTION

INTRODUCTION

1. *THESIS STATED*

IN the course of his opinion in *Missouri v. Holland*,[1] sustaining a treaty of the United States against the objection that its provisions invaded powers reserved to the States, Mr. Justice Holmes said:

When we are dealing with words that also are a constituent act like the Constitution of the United States, we must realize that they have called into life a being the development of which could not have been foreseen completely by the most gifted of its begetters. It was enough for them to realize or to hope that they had created an organism; it has taken a century and has cost their successors much sweat and blood to prove that they created a nation. The case before us must be considered in the light of our whole experience and not merely in that of what was said a hundred years ago. The treaty in question does not contravene any prohibitory words to be found in the Constitution. The only question is whether it is forbidden by some invisible radiation from the general terms of the Tenth Amendment. We must consider what this country has become in deciding what that Amendment has reserved.[2]

These words reflect a quite commonly entertained belief that national power has increased since 1789, from which the further conclusion

[1] 252 U.S. 416.
[2] *ibid.*, 433-4.

is often drawn that judicial review as administered by the Supreme Court has fostered this growth. Indeed, legal writers have not infrequently waxed enthusiastic over the liberality and wisdom of the Supreme Court in dealing out powers to the National Government as they were needed, the idea being apparently that the framers of the Constitution, having provided for the Court, called it a day and went home. When, nevertheless, proper distinctions are made, such ideas are found to be not altogether correct and such emotions not altogether called for, certainly so far as concerns the branch of national power herein dealt with.

The most important source of national power touching private conduct is, in ordinary times, the power of Congress to regulate commerce among the States. That the factual subject-matter hereby brought within the jurisdiction of the National Government is vastly greater today than it was in 1789 is of course obvious. What has escaped attention is that while the superficial *area* of national legislative power has thus expanded, its *depth* or *intensity*—in other words, *the discretion of Congress in its exercise*—is today far less than it was in constitutional law and theory, not only in 1789, but indeed throughout the first 100 years, substantially, of government under the Constitution.

This general thesis, however, can be stated more precisely. That commerce and industry have been largely reorganized since the middle 'eighties on a national scale no one would deny. Yet it is equally apparent that the natural outcome of this development for the distribution of power between the Nation and the States has not taken place. Why not? The answer is to be found, in important measure, in the hospitality of the Supreme Court in recent years toward theories regarding the nature of Congress's power over commerce among the States which go far toward stripping that power of its earlier attributes of sovereignty. In short, as the practical grounds for assertion by the National Government of its powers over interstate business relationship have expanded, the theoretical basis in constitutional law and theory for such assertion has deteriorated; and for this somewhat paradoxical situation the Supreme Court is to an important extent responsible.

2. *GIBBONS v. ODGEN, 1824*

The Constitution vests in Congress power *"to regulate Commerce with foreign nations, and among the several States, and with the Indian tribes"* (Article I, section 8, clause 3).

The first case to reach the Supreme Court which involved a construction of this clause was the famous "Steamboat Case," which was decided in 1824.[3] This litigation grew out of the conflict between a monopoly which the State of New York had conferred upon certain persons to navigate steamboats upon the waters of that State and an act of Congress regulating the coastwise trade. The case, therefore, raised directly the scope of Congress's power over *interstate commerce*.

Counsel for Ogden, in defending the monopoly, contended that the word "commerce" signified *traffic*, that is to say buying and selling (L. *cum merce*—with merchandise), together with such transportation as was purely auxiliary thereto. The Court, however, speaking by Chief Justice Marshall rejected this restrictive view in the following words:

Commerce undoubtedly is traffic, but it is something more; it is intercourse. . . .

It has, we believe, been universally admitted, that these words comprehend every species of intercourse between the United States and foreign nations. . . . If this be the admitted meaning of the word in its application to foreign nations it must carry the same meaning throughout the sentence, and remain a unit, unless there be some plain intelligible cause which alters it.[4]

The opinion then proceeds:

The subject to which the power is next applied is to commerce "among the several States." The word "among" means intermingled with. A thing which is among others is intermingled with them. Commerce

---

[3] 9 Wheat. 1.
[4] *ibid.*, 189, 193-4.

among the States cannot stop at the external boundary line of each State, but may be introduced into the interior.

It is not intended to say that these words comprehend that commerce which is completely internal, which is carried on between man and man in a State, or between different parts of the same State, and which does not extend to or affect other States. Such a power would be inconvenient and is certainly unnecessary.

Comprehensive as the word "among" is, it may very properly be restricted to that commerce which concerns more States than one. The phrase is not one which would probably have been selected to indicate the completely interior traffic of a State, because it is not an apt phrase for that purpose; and the enumeration of the particular classes of commerce to which the power was to be extended would not have been made had the intention been to extend the power to every description. The enumeration presupposes something not enumerated; and that something, if we regard the language or the subject of the sentence, must be the exclusively internal commerce of a State. The genius and character of the whole government seem to be, that its action is to be applied to all the external concerns of the Nation, and to those internal concerns which affect the States generally; but not to those which are completely within a particular State, which do not affect other States, and with which it is not necessary to interfere for the purpose of executing some of the general powers of the government. The completely internal commerce of a State, then, may be considered as reserved for the State itself.[5]

What, however, of Congress's power to *regulate?* Did the Act of 1793, confining the right to engage in the coastwise trade and the fish-

[5] *ibid.,* 194-5.

eries to vessels licensed under it, fall within the scope of this power? Marshall answered this question as follows:

We are now arrived at the inquiry—what is this power? It is the power to regulate; that is, to prescribe the rule by which commerce is to be governed. This power, like all others vested in Congress, is complete in itself, may be exercised to its utmost extent, and acknowledges no limitations, other than are prescribed in the Constitution. These are expressed in plain terms, and do not affect the questions which arise in this case, or which have been discussed at the bar. If, as has always been understood, the sovereignty of Congress, though limited to specified objects, is plenary as to those objects, the power over commerce with foreign nations, and among the several States, is vested in Congress as absolutely as it would be in a single government, having in its constitution the same restrictions on the exercise of the power as are found in the Constitution of the United States. The wisdom and the discretion of Congress, their identity with the people, and the influence which their constituents possess at elections, are, in this, as in many other instances, as that, for example, of declaring war, the sole restraints on which they have relied to secure them from its abuse. They are the restraints on which the people must often rely solely, in all representative governments.[6]

Later in the opinion the Chief Justice encountered a further objection to the act of Congress, and answered it as follows:

In pursuing this inquiry at the bar, it has been said, that the Constitution does not confer the right of intercourse between State and State. That right derives

[6] *ibid.*, 196-7.

its source from those laws whose authority is acknowledged by civilized man throughout the world. This is
true. The Constitution found it an existing right, and
gave Congress the power to regulate it. In the exercise
of this power, Congress has passed "an act for enrolling
or licensing ships or vessels to be employed in the
coasting trade and fisheries, and for regulating the
same." The counsel for the respondent contend, that
this act does not give the right to sail from port to
port, but confines itself to regulating a preexisting
right, so far only as to confer certain privileges on
enrolled and licensed vessels in its exercise.

It will at once occur, that, when a legislature
attaches certain privileges and exemptions to the
exercise of a right over which its control is absolute, the
law must imply a power to exercise the right. The
privileges are gone, if the right itself be annihilated.[7]

But it must not be supposed that Marshall,
while describing the national commercial
power in such sweeping terms, overlooked the
reserved powers of the States, or the competition thence arising with national power. Thus
referring to "inspection laws," he said:

They form a portion of that immense mass of
legislation, which embraces everything within the
territory of a State, not surrendered to the general
government; all which can be most advantageously
exercised by the States themselves. Inspection laws,
quarantine laws, health laws of every description, as
well as laws for regulating the internal commerce of
a State, and those which respect turnpike-roads,
ferries, etc., are component parts of this mass.[8]

[7] *ibid.*, 211-12.
[8] *ibid.*, 203.

The opinion then continues:

No direct general power over those objects is granted to Congress; and consequently, they remain subject to State legislation. If the legislative power of the Union can reach them, it must be for national purposes; it must be where the power is expressly given for a special purpose, or is clearly incidental to some power which is expressly given. . . .

In our complex system, presenting the rare and difficult scheme of one general government, whose action extends over the whole, but which possesses only certain enumerated powers; and of numerous State governments, which retain and exercise all powers not delegated to the Union, contests respecting power must arise. Were it even otherwise, the measures taken by the respective governments to execute their acknowledged powers, would often be of the same description, and might, sometimes, interfere.[9]

Proceeding from this basis, Marshall freely conceded the argument made for Ogden that New York might have created the monopoly which Gibbons was contesting, by virtue of its power to regulate its "domestic trade and police." But that fact, he promptly added, did not suffice to save the monopoly, since it con-flicted with a constitutional act of Congress regulatory of "commerce among the several States." He said:

In argument, however, it has been contended that if a law, passed by a State in the exercise of its acknowl-edged sovereignty, comes into conflict with a law passed by Congress in pursuance of the Constitution,

[9] *ibid.*, 203-5.

they affect the subject, and each other, like equal opposing powers.

But the framers of the Constitution foresaw this state of things, and provided for it, by declaring the supremacy not only of itself, but of the laws made in pursuance of it. The nullity of any act, inconsistent with the Constitution is produced by the declaration that the Constitution is the supreme law. The appropriate application of that part of the clause which confers the same supremacy on laws and treaties, is to such acts of the State legislatures as do not transcend their powers, but, though enacted in the execution of acknowledged State powers, interfere with, or are contrary to the laws of Congress made in pursuance of the Constitution, or some treaty made under the authority of the United States. In every such case, the act of Congress, or the treaty, is supreme; and the law of the State, though enacted in the exercise of powers not controverted, must yield to it.[10]

To sum up: Marshall in this opinion pictures Congress's powers to regulate commerce among the States as the power to *govern commercial intercourse* among them; and this power he characterizes as "sovereign," "complete," "plenary," "absolute," and of the same scope as it would be were it vested "in a single government." It is, in other words, unaffected by the coexistence of the States, and their powers. Finally, Congress's discretion in the exercise of this power, that is to say, in the selection of the purposes to be realized by its exercise, is limited only by that body's political respon-

[10] *ibid.*, 210-11.

sibility. The power is *not* in this aspect subject to judicial review.

And with this conception of the commercial power, Marshall's conception of State power was at all points harmonious. The States were conceded to have retained "an immense mass of legislation," including the power to govern their "completely internal commerce." But all State powers were conceived as subject to three important qualifications. In the first place, while national power is designed to extend "to all the external concerns of the Nation, and to those internal concerns which affect the States generally," the field of State power comprises only those internal concerns which are completely within a particular State and "do not affect other States." In the second place, however, even such completely internal concerns of a State may be interfered with by national power when such interference is necessary "for the purpose of executing some of the general powers of the government." Thirdly, no matter by what power it may have been enacted, any State law which conflicts with an otherwise constitutional act of Congress must yield to the latter.

The third is the point of controlling importance. It asserts that *when the supremacy clause is given its due operation no subject-matter whatever is withdrawn from the control of the delegated powers of the United States by the fact alone that the same subject-matter also lies within the jurisdiction of the reserved powers of the States; for when national and State power, correctly defined in all other respects, come into conflict in consequence of attempting to govern simultaneously the same subject-matter, the former has always the right of way.*

3. *HAMMER v. DAGENHART, 1918*

Chief Justice Marshall's opinion in *Gibbons v. Ogden* is the *terminus a quo* from which the argument of this volume sets out; the purposes of a *terminus ad quem* may, on the other hand, be served fairly satisfactorily by the decision of the Court ninety-four years later in the first Child Labor Case.[11] There by a vote of five Justices to four was held void an act of Congress prohibiting the interstate transportation of goods in the manufacture of which child labor had participated. Salient passages from Justice Day's opinion for the Court are the following:

In *Gibbons v. Ogden*, 9 Wheat. 1, Chief Justice Marshall, speaking for this Court, and defining the extent and nature of the commerce power, said, "It is the power to regulate; that is prescribe the rule by which commerce is to be governed." In other words, the power is one to control the means by which commerce is carried on, which is directly contrary of the assumed right to forbid commerce from moving and thus destroy it as to particular commodities.[12]

[11] *Hammer v. Dagenhart*, 247 U.S. 251 (1918).
[12] *ibid.*, 269-70.

To be sure, Justice Day conceded, there had been prohibitions upon transportation between the States which the Court had sustained, but he continued:

In each of these instances the use of interstate transportation was necessary to the accomplishment of harmful results. In other words, although the power over interstate transportation was to regulate, that could only be accomplished by prohibiting the use of the facilities of interstate commerce to effect the evil intended.[13]

He then stated what he considered to be the main vice of the act under review—that it undertook to regulate a matter which was subject to State control, production, to wit. He said:

The grant of power to Congress over the subject of interstate commerce was to enable it to regulate such commerce, and not to give it authority to control the States in the exercise of the police power over local trade and manufacture.

The grant of authority over a purely federal matter was not intended to destroy the local power always existing and carefully reserved to the States in the Tenth Amendment to the Constitution. . . .

A statute must be judged by its natural and reasonable effect. *Collins v. New Hampshire*, 171 U.S. 30, 33, 34. The control by Congress over interstate commerce cannot authorize the exercise of authority not entrusted to it by the Constitution. *Pipe Line Cases*, 234 U.S. 548, 560. The maintenance of the authority of the States over matters purely local is as essential to the preservation of our institutions as is the conservation

[13] *ibid.*, 271.

of the supremacy of the federal power in all matters
entrusted to the Nation by the Federal Constitution.

In interpreting the Constitution it must never be
forgotten that the Nation is made up of States to which
are entrusted the powers of local government. And to
them and to the people the powers not expressly delegated to the National Government are reserved. *Lane
County v. Oregon*, 7 Wall. 71, 76. The power of the
States to regulate their purely internal affairs by such
laws as seem wise to the local authority is inherent and
has never been surrendered to the general government.
New York v. Miln, 11 Pet. 102, 139; *Slaughter House
Cases*, 16 Wall. 36, 63; *Kidd v. Pearson, supra*. To sustain this statute would not be in our judgment a recognition of the lawful exertion of congressional authority
over interstate commerce, but would sanction an
invasion by the federal power of the control of a matter
purely local in its character, and over which no
authority has been delegated to Congress in conferring
the power to regulate commerce among the States.[14]

To this line of reasoning, Justice Holmes,
speaking for himself and Justices McKenna,
Brandeis, and Clarke, replied as follows:

The first step in my argument is to make plain what
no one is likely to dispute—that the statute in question
is within the power expressly given to Congress if considered only as to its immediate effects and that if invalid it is so only upon some collateral ground. The
statute confines itself to prohibiting the carriage of
certain goods in interstate or foreign commerce. Congress is given power to regulate such commerce in
unqualified terms. It would not be argued today that
the power to regulate does not include the power to
prohibit. Regulation means the prohibition of something, and when interstate commerce is the matter to

[14] *ibid.*, 274-6.

be regulated I cannot doubt that the regulation may prohibit any part of such commerce that Congress sees fit to forbid. . . .

The question then is narrowed to whether the exercise of its otherwise constitutional power by Congress can be pronounced unconstitutional because of its possible reaction upon the conduct of the States in a matter upon which I have admitted that they are free from direct control. I should have thought that that matter had been disposed of so fully as to leave no room for doubt. I should have thought that the most conspicuous decisions of this Court had made it clear that the power to regulate commerce and other constitutional powers could not be cut down or qualified by the fact that it might interfere with the carrying out of the domestic policy of any State. . . .

The notion that prohibition is any less prohibition when applied to things now thought evil I do not understand. But if there is any matter upon which civilized countries have agreed—far more unanimously than they have with regard to intoxicants and some other matters over which this country is now emotionally aroused—it is the evil of premature and excessive child labor. I should have thought that if we were to introduce our own moral conceptions where in my opinion they do not belong, this was preeminently a case for upholding the exercise of all its powers by the United States.

But I had thought that the propriety of the exercise of a power admitted to exist in some cases was for the consideration of Congress alone and that this Court always had disavowed the right to intrude its judgment upon questions of policy or morals. It is not for this Court to pronounce when prohibition is necessary to regulation if it ever may be necessary—to say that it is permissible as against strong drink but not so against the product of ruined lives.

The act does not meddle with anything belonging to the States. They may regulate their internal affairs and their domestic commerce as they like. But when they seek to send their products across the State line they are no longer within their rights. If there were no Constitution and no Congress their power to cross the line would depend upon their neighbors. Under the Constitution such commerce belongs not to the States but to Congress to regulate. It may carry out its views of public policy whatever indirect effect they may have upon the activities of the States. Instead of being encountered by a prohibitive tariff at her boundaries the State encounters the public policy of the United States which it is for Congress to express. The public policy of the United States is shaped with a view to the benefit of the Nation as a whole. If, as has been the case within the memory of men still living, a State should take a different view of the propriety of sustaining a lottery from that which generally prevails, I cannot believe that the fact would require a different decision from that reached in *Champion v. Ames*. Yet in that case it would be said with quite as much force as in this that Congress was attempting to intermeddle with the State's domestic affairs. The national welfare as understood by Congress may require a different attitude within its sphere from that of some self-seeking State. It seems to me entirely constitutional for Congress to enforce its understanding by all the means at its command.[15]

4. *SIX PROPOSITIONS*

The question that necessarily arises upon a comparison of Marshall's opinion in *Gibbons v. Ogden* and Day's opinion in *Hammer v. Dagenhart* is, how did the Court ever get from the one to the other—what were the steps?

[15] *ibid.*, 277-81.

The answer is, that there were no *steps*. The method of the Court was nothing so pedestrian. Rather is it to be compared to that of those Chinese rivers which occasionally abandon the courses they have followed for decades and proceed to plow a new channel to the sea, at sharp angles to the first. Only in the case of the Court, while a new channel was cut, the old one also continued in use. The once impressive current of harmonious doctrine was abruptly cleft into two lesser currents flowing in opposite directions.

To speak more precisely, while the decision in *Hammer v. Dagenhart* is shockingly lacking in *precedential antecedents*, it does have certain *doctrinal antecedents*; and it will be the main task of this book to evaluate these. For this is not a case, fortunately, in which *"rechercher la paternité est interdit."* The doctrinal antecedents referred to comprise, or at least may be summed up in, the following propositions:

(1) That the framers of the Constitution conferred upon Congress the power to regulate commerce among the States with a different intent than the power to regulate foreign commerce, with the result that the former power is of less scope than the latter power;

(2) That the power to regulate commerce among the States does not include the power to prohibit it;

(3) That while Congress has power to restrain commerce among the States for the benefit of such commerce, this power is not available for the promotion of the general welfare in other respects;

(4) That the reserved powers of the States constitute a limitation upon Congress's power to regulate commerce among the States and serve to withdraw certain matters from the jurisdiction of the latter power;

(5) That production is a subject which is segregated to the reserved powers of the States, and so lies outside the range of Congress's power to regulate commerce among the States;

(6) That Congress's purpose in enacting a measure is a judicially enforcible test of the validity of such measure if it invades the ordinary domain of the States.

Proposition (3), it should be added, is a post-Civil war variant of Proposition (2), while Proposition (5) is the form in which Proposition (4) is currently important. The ensuing chapters will set forth, mainly by means of quotations from judicial opinions, arguments of counsel, and authoritative writers the record of discussion on each of these propositions, interlarding the material given with relevant comments.

CHAPTER TWO
PROPOSITION I

PROPOSITION I

That the power of Congress to regulate commerce among the States is of less scope than its power to regulate commerce with foreign nations.

1. *THE MADISONIAN DOCTRINE OF 1829*

THE two considerations which were foremost in the minds of the framers of the Constitution when they conferred the commercial power upon Congress were, first, the helplessness of the United States in dealing with foreign nations because of the dispersion of the commercial power under the Articles of Confederation among the States; and secondly, the hostility which had arisen among the States because of their restrictive measures directed against one another's commerce. The two immediate objectives back of the commerce clause were, accordingly, these: (1) to enable the National Government to deal with foreign nations as a unit respecting commerce; (2) to bring to an end either directly or through Congressional action, all State power in relation to both foreign and interstate commerce. And the two objectives were accomplished by the simple method of conferring on Congress the power to regulate commerce with foreign nations and among the several States: in other words, by an unqualified grant of power in both instances, not by a grant of power in the one instance and a prohibition upon the States in the other, though nothing could have been easier than to adopt the latter course had it been preferred. But in fact nobody suggested such a solution, either in the proposals for amending the Articles of Confederation between the years 1781 and 1787, or in the Convention.

The question accordingly arises whether this diversity of *immediate objective* as regards the two branches of the commercial power affords a canon of constitutional interpretation which may be validly applied for rendering nugatory Congress's power over commerce among the States. The idea that it did is generally traceable to a letter written by James Madison to J. C. Cabell, February 13, 1829, and so some five years after the decision in *Gibbons v. Ogden*. Madison there said:

I always foresaw that difficulties might be started in relation to that power which could not be fully explained without recurring to views of it, which, however just, might give birth to specious though unsound objections. Being in the same terms with the power over foreign commerce, the same extent, if taken literally, would belong to it. Yet it is very certain that it grew out of the abuse of the power by the importing States in taxing the non-importing, and was intended as a negative and preventive provision against injustice among the States themselves, rather than as a power to be used for the positive purposes of the General Government, in which alone, however, the remedial power could be lodged. And it will be safer to leave the power with this key to it, than to extend to it all the qualities and incidental means belonging to the power over foreign commerce, as is unavoidable, according to the reasoning I see applied to the case.[1]

The paradoxical nature of this theory is evident on a moment's reflection. It is contended, in effect, that the grant of power to Congress to regulate commerce among the States merely took this power from the States without vesting the equivalent power in Congress. The net result of the transfer is therefore that both the States from which the power was taken and Congress to which it was in explicit terms given, have equal power to regulate commerce among the States "for positive purposes"—which is to say, *no power*. "The power perished as the result of the act by which it was conferred."[2] But as was pointed out above, if the framers intended such a result the logical way for them to achieve it would have been to impose a simple prohibition on the States; and at least they might reasonably be expected to have avoided the precise phrase which they would have employed had they sought the directly contrary result—which in fact, they *did* employ when they conferred on Congress the power

---

[1] *Letters and Other Writings of James Madison* (1867), IV, 14-15.
[2] Chief Justice White, in 234 U.S. 476, 493.

to regulate foreign commerce "for the positive purposes of the General Government"!

Nor does the fact that the interstate commerce clause today comprises a limitation on State power, on the theory that the power thus granted Congress is "exclusive," help Madison's argument out, for the same doctrine holds even more rigorously as to Congress's power over foreign commerce. Indeed, the exclusiveness of Congress's power in the latter respect was established in our Constitution a quarter of a century before the exclusiveness of its power over interstate commerce. Not until 1851, that is to say, more than sixty years after the adoption of the Constitution, did the negative purpose, which Madison asserted to be the *sole* purpose, of the grant to Congress of power over interstate commerce, receive the Court's confirmation.[3]

The fact of the matter is that nothing was said in the Convention of 1787 of which record remains that in any wise justifies Madison's statement to Cabell; nor was anything said while ratification was pending, but much to the contrary, as will be pointed out in the next chapter. Prior indeed to the Convention Madison himself went on record for a very different view of the power which would result to the General Government from the right to regulate commerce among the States.

[3] In *Cooley v. Port Wardens*, 12 How. 299.

Thus, in a letter to Washington, dated April 16, 1787, and so written only a few weeks before the assembling of the Convention, he said: "The National Government should be armed with positive and complete authority in all cases which require uniformity; such as the regulation of trade . . ."; and further along he added: "With the resources of commerce in hand, the national administration might always find means for asserting it [the power of coercion upon the States] whether by land or sea," although he deprecated such means, suggesting instead a negative on State laws.[4]

Also in *Federalist No. XIV*, we find him writing:

Let it be remarked, in the third place, that the intercourse throughout the Union will be facilitated by new improvements. Roads will everywhere be shortened, and kept in better order; accommodations for travellers will be multiplied and meliorated; an interior navigation on our eastern side will be opened throughout, or nearly throughout, the whole extent of the thirteen States. The communication between the Western and Atlantic districts, and between different parts of each, will be rendered more and more easy by those numerous canals with which the beneficence of nature has intersected our country and which art finds it so little difficult to connect and complete.[5]

This seems to be a promise or prediction that the new government would actively foster

[4] *Writings* (Hunt, Ed.), II, 345, 346, 348.
[5] Lodge, Ed., 80.

commerce among the States by providing facilities for it. On this point, however, as on so many others, Madison later recanted, and the Cabell letter is simply a somewhat more elaborate statement of the doctrine of his veto of March 3, 1817, of the so-called "Bonus Bill," devoting certain funds to internal improvements.[6]

Finally, it does not appear that Madison even in 1829 regarded his theory of the negative purpose of the interstate commerce clause as stating a really authoritative canon of constitutional construction. Thus in a letter to N. P. Trist, written in December 1831, he said:

Another error has been in ascribing to the *intention* of the *Convention* which formed the Constitution, an undue ascendency in expounding it. Apart from the difficulty of verifying that intention, it is clear, that if the meaning of the Constitution is to be sought out of itself, it is not in the proceedings of the body that proposed it, but in those of the State Conventions, which gave it all the validity and authority it possesses.[7]

And earlier he had written: "The legitimate meaning of the Instrument must be derived from the text itself"[8]—a statement thoroughly

[6] Richardson, Ed., *Messages and Papers of the Presidents*, I, 584.

[7] *Letters and Other Writings*, IV, 211. In just what way it would be easier to ascertain the intention of the numerous ratifying conventions than that of the Convention which framed the Constitution is, unfortunately, a point upon which Madison does not enlighten us.

[8] *ibid.*, III, 228. It must be admitted, however, that Madison seems, at one time or other, to have given his approval to about

in harmony with the Court's declaration nearly eighty years later, when confronted with the doctrine of the Cabell letter: "The reasons which may have caused the framers to repose the powers to regulate interstate commerce in Congress do not, however, affect or limit the extent of the power itself."[9]

Moreover, being put the question "whether, as the power to regulate commerce between the States is in the same words with that to regulate it with foreign nations," a protective tariff, which he favored, against the products of other nations would not authorize one between the States, Madison accompanied his reiteration of the negative character of the interstate commerce power, with these significant words:

Waiving the constitutional obstacles . . . the difficulties, the futility, and the odium of such a project would be a sufficient security against it; a better security then can be found against abuses to most of the powers vested in every government.[10]

Also, it was a favorite maxim with Madison that "the powers [of the United States and the States] taken together, ought to be equal to all of the objects of government, not specially excepted for special reasons, as in the case of

every rule which any one has ever stated for construing the Constitution.

[9] Justice Peckham, speaking for the Court, in *Addyston Pipe and Steel Co. v. U.S.*, 175 U.S. 211, 228 (1899).

[10] *Letters and Other Writings*, IV, 257.

duties on exports."[11] But obviously if the doctrine of the Cabell letter is sound, then the above maxim is not sound, for by that doctrine, the power over commerce among the States "perished as the result of the act by which it was conferred."[12]

Returning to the period of the adoption of the Constitution, it is to be observed that Hamilton, in the *Federalist*, discussed Congress's powers over commerce in his usual sweeping terms, and without any hint of recognition that there was a difference between the two branches of the power. His words are:

The principal purposes to be answered by union are these—the common defense of the members; the preservation of the public peace, as well against internal convulsions as external attacks; the regulation of commerce with other nations and between the States; the superintendence of our intercourse, political and commercial, with foreign countries. . . . Shall the Union be constituted the guardian of the common safety? Are fleets and armies and revenues necessary to this purpose? The government of the Union must be empowered to pass all laws, and to make all regulations which have relation to them. The same must be the case in respect to commerce, and to every other matter to which its jurisdiction is permitted to extend.[13]

Arguing two years later in favor of his Bank proposal, Hamilton declared that Congress, under the commerce clause, could create cor-

---

[11] *ibid.*, IV, 250; also to same effect, III, 640, 644, 654.
[12] Note 2, *supra*.
[13] No. 23; Lodge, Ed., 136-8 *passim*.

porations to carry on foreign trade between the States and with the Indians.[14]

2. *JUDICIAL OPINION TO 1904*

The record of judicial opinion will now be canvassed. To the passages earlier given from Chief Justice Marshall's opinion in *Gibbons v. Ogden*, it is pertinent to add the following extracts from Justice Johnson's separate opinion in that case:

The "power to regulate commerce," here meant to be granted, was that power to regulate commerce which previously existed in the States. But what was that power? The States were, unquestionably, supreme; and each possessed that power over commerce, which is acknowledged to reside in every sovereign State. The definition and limits of that power are to be sought among the features of international law; and, as it was not only admitted, but insisted on by both parties, in argument, that, "unaffected by a state of war, by treaties, or by municipal regulations, all commerce among independent States was legitimate," there is no necessity to appeal to the oracles of the *jus commune* for the correctness of that doctrine. The law of nations, regarding man as a social animal, pronounces all commerce legitimate, in a state of peace, until prohibited by positive law. The power of a sovereign State over commerce, therefore, amounts to nothing more than a power to limit and restrain it at pleasure. And since the power to prescribe the limits to its freedom, necessarily implies the power to determine what shall remain unrestrained, it follows, that the power must be exclusive; it can reside but in one potentate; and hence, the grant

[14] *Works* (Lodge, Ed.), III, 184-5.

of this power carries with it the whole subject, leaving nothing for the State to act upon. . . .

Power to regulate foreign commerce is given in the same words, and in the same breath, as it were, with that over the commerce of the States and with the Indian tribes. But the power to regulate foreign commerce is necessarily exclusive. The States are unknown to foreign nations; their sovereignty exists only with relation to each other and the general government. Whatever regulations foreign commerce should be subjected to in the ports of the Union, the general government would be held responsible for them; and all other regulations, but those which Congress had imposed, would be regarded by foreign nations as trespasses and violations of national faith and comity.

But the language which grants the power as to one description of commerce, grants it as to all; and, in fact, if ever the exercise of a right, or acquiescence in a construction, could be inferred from contemporaneous and continued assent, it is that of the exclusive effect of this grant. A right over the subject has never been pretended to, in any instance, except as incidental to exercise of some other unquestionable power.[15]

In short, *Congress's power over foreign commerce is the measure and test of its power over commerce among the States.* Apparently the only utterance from the Supreme Bench prior to 1901 reflecting the Madisonian distinction between Congress's power over foreign and interstate commerce is a dictum from Justice McLean's individual opinion in *Groves v. Slaughter*,[16] which is quoted in the following chapter.

[15] 9 Wheat. 1, 227-9 *passim*.
[16] 15 Pet. 449, 505 (1841).

Here follows a series of judicial dicta from opinions of the Court, traversing a period of over fifty years, every one of which asserts the equal scope of Congress's power over interstate and foreign commerce:

(1) The power to regulate commerce among the several States is granted to Congress in the same clause, and by the same words, as the power to regulate commerce with foreign nations, and is coextensive with it.[17]

(2) The power to "regulate commerce," conferred by the Constitution upon Congress, is that which previously existed in the States.[18]

(3) Power over one is given by the Constitution of the United States to Congress in the same words in which it is given over the other, and in both cases it is necessarily exclusive.[19]

(4) The power to regulate commerce among the several States is granted to Congress in terms as absolute as is the power to regulate commerce with foreign nations. If not in all respects an exclusive power; if, in the absence of Congressional action, the States may continue to regulate matters of local interest only incidentally affecting foreign and interstate commerce, such as pilots, wharves, harbors, roads, bridges, tolls, freights, etc., still, according to the rule laid down in *Cooley v. Board of Wardens of Philadelphia*, 12 How. 299, 319, the power of Congress is exclusive wherever the matter is national in its character or admits of one uniform system or plan of regulation.[20]

(5) The power conferred upon Congress to regulate commerce among the States is indeed contained in the same clause of the Constitution which confers upon it power to regulate commerce with foreign nations. The

[17] C. J. Taney, *License Cases*, 5 How. 504, 578 (1847).
[18] J. Strong, *South Carolina v. Ga. et al*; 93 U.S. 4, 10 (1876).
[19] Same, *Railroad Co. v. Husen*, 95 U.S. 465, 469 (1877).
[20] J. Bradley, *Brown v. Houston*, 114 U.S. 622, 630 (1885).

grant is conceived in the same terms, and the two powers are undoubtedly of the same class and character and equally extensive. The actual exercise of its power over either subject is equally and necessarily exclusive of that of the States; and paramount over all the powers of the States; so that State legislation, however legitimate in its origin or object, when it conflicts with the positive legislation of Congress, or its intention reasonably implied from its silence, in respect to the subject of commerce of both kinds, must fail. And yet in respect to the subject of commerce among the States, it may be for the reason already assigned, that the same inference is not always to be drawn from the absence of Congressional legislation as might be in the case of commerce with foreign nations. The question, therefore, may be still considered in each case as it arises, whether the fact that Congress has failed in the particular instance to provide by law a regulation of commerce among the States is conclusive of its intention that the subject shall be free from all positive regulation, or that, until it positively interferes, such commerce may be left to be freely dealt with by the respective States.[21]

(6) It has frequently been laid down by this Court that the power of Congress over interstate commerce is as absolute as it is over foreign commerce. Would any one pretend that a State legislature could prohibit a foreign corporation—an English or a French transportation company, for example—from coming into its borders and landing goods and passengers at its wharves, and soliciting goods and passengers for a return voyage, without first obtaining a license from some State officer, and filing a sworn statement as to the amount of its capital stock paid in? And why not? Evidently because the matter is not within the province of State legislation, but within that of national legislation. *Inman*

[21] J. Matthews, *Bowman v. Chic. and N. W. R. Co.*, 125 U.S. 465, 482-3 (1888).

Steamship Co. v. Tinker, 94 U.S. 238. The prerogative, the responsibility and the duty of providing for the security of the citizens and the people of the United States in relation to foreign corporate bodies, or foreign individuals with whom they may have relations of foreign commerce, belong to the government of the United States, and not to the governments of the several States; and confidence in that regard may be reposed in the national legislature without any anxiety or apprehension arising from the fact that the subject matter is not within the province or jurisdiction of the State legislatures. And the same thing is exactly true with regard to interstate commerce as it is with regard to foreign commerce. No difference is perceivable between the two. *Telegraph Co. v. Texas*, 105 U.S. 460; *Gloucester Ferry Co. v. Pennsylvania*, 114 U.S. 196, 205, 211; *Phila. Steamship Co. v. Pennsylvania*, 122 U.S. 326, 342; *McCall v. California*, 136 U.S. 104, 110; *Norfolk & Western Railroad v. Pennsylvania*, 136 U.S. 114, 118.[22]

(7) The power to regulate commerce among the several States was granted to Congress in terms as absolute as is the power to regulate commerce with foreign nations.[23]

Furthermore, on three occasions when the Court was squarely confronted with the Madisonian thesis, it rejected it. The first occasion was in 1891, in the case of *in re Rahrer*.[24] Said Chief Justice Fuller, speaking for the Court:

(8) It is earnestly contended that the Constitution guarantees the freedom of commerce among the States in all things. . . .

[22] J. Bradley, *Crutcher v. Ky.*, 141 U.S. 47, 57-8 (1891).
[23] J. Field, *Pittsburgh, etc. Coal Co. v. Bates*, 156 U.S. 577, 587 (1895).
[24] 140 U.S. 545.

Thus the grant to the general government of a power designed to prevent embarrassing restrictions upon interstate commerce by any State, would be made to forbid any restraint whatever. We do not concur in this view. In surrendering their own power over external commerce the States did not secure absolute freedom in such commerce, but only the protection from encroachment afforded by confiding its regulation exclusively to Congress.

By the adoption of the Constitution the ability of the several States to act upon the matter solely in accordance with their own will was extinguished, and the legislative will of the general government substituted. No affirmative guaranty was thereby given to any State of the right to demand as between it and the others what it could not have obtained before; while the object was undoubtedly sought to be attained of preventing commercial regulations partial in their character or contrary to the common interests. And the magnificent growth and prosperity of the country attest the success which has attended the accomplishment of that object. But this furnishes no support to the position that Congress could not, in the exercise of the discretion reposed in it, concluding that the common interests did not require entire freedom in the traffic in ardent spirits, enact the law in question.[25]

The second such occasion was in 1895 in the famous Sugar Trust Case.[26] Said Chief Justice Fuller, speaking for the Court:

(9) The Constitution does not provide that interstate commerce shall be free, but, by the grant of this exclusive power to regulate it, it was left free except as Congress might impose restraints. Therefore it has been determined that the failure of Congress to exer-

[25] *ibid.*, 561.
[26] *United States v. E. C. Knight Co.*, 156 U.S. 1.

cise this exclusive power in any case is an expression of its will that the subject shall be free from restrictions or impositions upon it by the several States. And if a law passed by a State in the exercise of its acknowledged powers comes into conflict with that will, the Congress and the State cannot occupy the position of equal opposing sovereignties, because the Constitution declares its supremacy and that of the laws passed in pursuance thereof; and that which is not supreme must yield to that which is supreme.[27]

The third time when the Court confronted the Madisonian argument and rejected it was in *Addyston Pipe and Steel Co. v. U.S.*[28] Said Justice Peckham on that occasion:

(10) Assuming, for the purpose of the argument, that the contract in question herein does directly and substantially operate as a restraint upon and as a regulation of interstate commerce, it is yet insisted by the appellants at the threshold of the inquiry that by the true construction of the Constitution, the power of Congress to regulate interstate commerce is limited to its protection from acts of interference by State legislation or by means of regulations made under the authority of the State by some political subdivision thereof. . . .

This argument is founded upon the assertion that the reason for vesting in Congress the power to regulate commerce was to insure uniformity of regulation against conflicting and discriminating State legislation; and the further assertion that the Constitution guarantees liberty of private contract to the citizen, at least upon commercial subjects, and to that extent the guaranty operates as a limitation on the power of Congress to regulate commerce. . . .

[27] *ibid.*, 11-12.
[28] 175 U.S. 211 (1899).

It is undoubtedly true that among the reasons, if not the strongest reason, for placing the power in Congress to regulate interstate commerce, was that which is stated in the extracts from the opinions of the Court in the cases above cited. . .

The reasons which may have caused the framers of the Constitution to repose the power to regulate interstate commerce in Congress do not, however, affect or limit the extent of the power itself. . . .

While unfriendly or discriminating legislation of the several States may have been the chief cause for granting to Congress the sole power to regulate interstate commerce, yet we fail to find in the language of the grant any such limitation of that power as would exclude Congress from legislating on the subject and prohibiting those private contracts which would directly and substantially, and not as a mere incident, regulate interstate commerce.

If certain kinds of private contracts do directly, as already stated, limit or restrain, and hence regulate, interstate commerce, why should not the power of Congress reach those contracts just the same as if the legislation of some State had enacted the provisions contained in them? The private contracts may in truth be as far-reaching in their effect upon interstate commerce as would the legislation of a single State of the same character.[29]

3. THE MADISONIAN REVIVAL

For the revival of the Madisonian thesis within recent years four reasons may be assigned. The first and most important, is the fact that it provides such an admirable vehicle, constructed from the very terminology of Constitutional law and theory, for industrial *lais-*

[29] *ibid.*, 226-30.

sez faire-ism, denying as it does to *both* the National Government and the States any power to *restrain* commerce among the States. Secondly, and by the same sign, it enlarges the supervisory rôle of the Court in relation to the national legislative powers, and so appeals directly to the Court's liking for power. Thirdly, it lent Justice (later Chief Justice) White, a former soldier of the Confederacy, a most convenient weapon in his crusade for "dual federalism" and against that extension of the powers of the National Government which the commercial and industrial nationalization of the country seemed to indicate was near at hand. Finally, by a curious chance, the Madisonian thesis underwent, at the turn of the century, a *literary revival*, in Mr. John Randolph Tucker's two volume work on *The Constitution of the United States*, which appeared posthumously in 1899. Tucker's theory of the nature of the Union appears in the following passages from this work:

The Union is *Staaten-bund*—not *Bundes-staat*. Each State is a republic of which the units are men. The United States is a confederate union, of which the units are not men but States. The States still exist as primordial Bodies-politic, and by their organic union they are a confederation of States—a Republic of Republics—but not a new composite, or one new civil Body-politic. . . .

What is the nature of the government of the United States established by the Constitution? . . . It is a federal government throughout, in whose organism

States are factors, and through which the States as such act with their combined powers. In this sense it may be averred that there is no department of the government of the United States, and no function thereof, which is not mediately or immediately impelled or directed by State authority.[30]

It was said of the Bourbons that they never learned anything and never forgot anything, and it is the same with the convinced States-Righter. Here, in condensed form, is the whole law and gospel of the Virginia and Kentucky Resolutions except the logically necessary corollary thereof that the final authority in interpreting the Constitution rests with the individual States. Not even the Civil War meant anything to Mr. Tucker, and much less did the nationalization of the country in every other respect save that of governmental authority. That he should attempt to pull the Madisonian doctrine concerning Congress's power to regulate commerce among the States out of its mummy case and make it speak again, is therefore in no wise surprising. The surprising thing is the degree of success with which this hocus-pocus has met.

The following passages from Tucker's treatise are pertinent in this connection:

In regulating commerce, therefore, Congress regulates traffic in things, vehicles of transport, and things in transit, but not the things themselves. Before and after the transitus they are beyond this power of regu-

[30] Tucker, J. R., *The Constitution of the United States* (1899), I, 318.

lation. The production and use of things in the *terminus a quo* and the *terminus ad quem* are not subjects of the commercial power, but of the law of the State or country from which and to which they are transported.

But does the power so extensive in its reach as to foreign commerce have the same interpretation as to interstate commerce? A negative answer must be given to this question. The considerations which justify this conclusion are too important to be omitted.

(a) Under the Articles of Confederation the States could interdict trade *inter se*. The grant of power to Congress to regulate interstate commerce was with the purpose not to transfer this power of interdicting interstate trade to Congress, but to leave interstate commerce free, as the Constitution intended, in order to form a more perfect union. Could the Constitution have intended to destroy the freedom of interstate trade by Congressional power when it took it from the States and vested it in Congress in order to prevent such destruction?

When we look at all powers vested in Congress as trust powers to be used for the States as beneficiaries and as members of one family of Commonwealths, so to be used as to promote union and not disunion, to establish harmony and peace and not discord and hostility between the States, it must be inevitably predicted that the courts will never hold any law of Congress which prohibits, restricts, or ties interstate commerce to be either necessary or proper as a regulation of commerce, but they must hold it to be a perversion of its trust power to the subversion of the fundamental principles of the Constitution. The power to regulate foreign and interstate commerce was given in the same terms *diverso intuitu*. In the first, to protect all against the machinations of foreign enemies; in the second, to protect and promote the free and unobstructed movement of men and things between the States in the family of the Union.[31]

These considerations conclusively show that the power to regulate interstate commerce is not commensurate with the power of Congress to regulate foreign commerce. . . . The whole Constitution, in all its parts, looks to the security of free trade in persons and goods between the States of the Union, and . . . prohibits either Congress or the States to interfere with this freedom of intercourse and trade.[32]

"All powers vested in Congress" are "trust powers to be used for the States as beneficiaries"—this belated re-echo of the extreme States-Rightism of some of the opinions in the Dred Scott Case serves to date Tucker's point of view most satisfactorily.

The influence of Tucker's work with the Court first appears in two *dissenting* opinions, both penned, it is instructive to note, by Chief Justice Fuller, who a few years previously had rejected the Madisonian teaching with emphasis in his opinion for the Court in Rahrer's Case and in the Sugar Trust Case, as we noted earlier.

The first of these dissents occurred in 1901, in connection with *Dooley v. United States*.[33] The apposite portion follows:

But if that power of regulation is absolutely unrestricted as respects interstate commerce, then the very unity the Constitution was framed to secure can be set

[31] *ibid.*, II, 528-9.
[32] *ibid.*, 533.
[33] 183 U.S. 151.

at naught by a legislative body created by that instrument.

Such a conclusion is wholly inadmissible. The power to regulate interstate commerce was granted in order that trade between the States might be left free from discriminating legislation and not to impart the power to create antagonistic commercial relations between them.

The prohibition of preference of ports was coupled with the prohibition of taxation on articles exported. The citizens of each State were declared "entitled to all privileges and immunities of citizens in the several States," and that included the right of ingress and egress and the enjoyment of the privileges of trade and commerce.[34]

The other dissent referred to occurred two years later in the famous Lottery Case.[35] The passage referred to is the following:

It is argued that the power to regulate commerce among the several States is the same as the power to regulate commerce with foreign nations, and among the Indian tribes. But is its scope the same? . . .

The power to regulate commerce with foreign nations and the power to regulate interstate commerce, are to be taken *diverso intuitu*, for the latter was intended to secure equality and freedom in commercial intercourse as between the States, not to permit the creation of impediments to such intercourse, while the former clothes Congress with that power over international commerce, pertaining to a sovereign nation in its intercourse with foreign nations, and subject, generally speaking, to no implied or reserved power in the States. The laws which would be necessary and proper in the one case would not be necessary or proper in the other. . . .

[34] *ibid.*, 171-2.
[35] 188 U.S. 321.

But that does not challenge the legislative power of a sovereign nation to exclude foreign persons or commodities, or place an embargo, perhaps not permanent, upon foreign ships or manufactures. . . .

The same view must be taken as to commerce with Indian tribes. There is no reservation of police powers or any other to a foreign nation, or to an Indian tribe, and the scope of the power is not the same as that over interstate commerce.[36]

And at this point the torch of the new illumination passed to Justice White. In *Buttfield v. Stranahan*,[37] a case involving only foreign commerce, White seized the occasion to cast a doubt upon the equal scope of Congress's power over the two principal branches of Commerce, in the following language:

The power to regulate commerce with foreign nations is expressly conferred upon Congress, and being an enumerated power is complete in itself, acknowledging no limitations other than those prescribed in the Constitution. *Lottery Case*, 188 U.S. 321, 353-6; *Leisy v. Hardin*, 135 U.S. 100, 108. Whatever difference of opinion, if any, may have existed or does exist concerning the limitations of the power, resulting from other provisions of the Constitution, so far as interstate commerce is concerned, it is not to be doubted

---

[36] *ibid.*, 373-4. Further evidence of Tucker's influence is afforded by a report from the Judiciary Committee of the House, in 1906, which condemned on constitutional grounds certain proposals of President Theodore Roosevelt looking to restrictive legislation on corporations engaged in interstate commerce: "He [Tucker] wrote at a time when there was nothing being said about it by the general public. His mind was perfectly free to follow his convictions and understanding of the law." This is said with direct reference to Tucker's views on the commerce power. *H. R. No. 2491*, 59th Cong., 1st Sess.

[37] 192 U.S. 470 (1904).

that from the beginning Congress has exercised a plenary power in respect to the exclusion of merchandise brought from foreign countries; not alone directly by the enactment of embargo statutes, but indirectly as a necessary result of provisions contained in tariff legislation. It has also, in other than tariff legislation, exerted a police power over foreign commerce by provisions which in and of themselves amounted to the assertion of the right to exclude merchandise at discretion. This is illustrated by statutory provisions which have been in force for more than fifty years, regulating the degree of strength of drugs, medicines and chemicals entitled to admission into the United States and excluding such as did not equal the standards adopted. 9 Stat. 237; Rev. Stat. sec. 2933 *et seq*.

The power to regulate foreign commerce is certainly as efficacious as that to regulate commerce with the Indian tribes. And this last power was referred to in *United States v. 43 Gallons of Whiskey*, 93 U.S. 188, 194, as exclusive and absolute, and was declared to be "as broad and as free from restrictions as that to regulate commerce with foreign nations."[38]

It should be noted in passing that the two cases which Justice White here cites in support of Congress's plenary power over foreign commerce, had actually to do only with commerce among the States. But the doubt thus subtly insinuated as to the scope of Congress's power over commerce among the States becomes eight years later, in the case of the *Abby Dodge*,[39] the reason assigned for holding that an act of Congress which regulated the landing of sponges at ports of the United States

[38] *ibid.*, 492-3.
[39] 223 U.S. 166 (1912).

related only to sponges taken outside the
territory of the United States.[40] Finally in
Brolan v. United States,[41] in which the right of
Congress to forbid the importation of opium
into the United States was sustained, implication is replaced by explication in the following
words:

In the argument reference is made to decisions of
this Court dealing with the subject of the power of Congress to regulate interstate commerce, but the very
postulate upon which the authority of Congress to
absolutely prohibit foreign importations as expounded
by the decisions of this Court rests is the broad distinction which exists between the two powers and therefore the cases cited and many more which might be
cited announcing the principles which they uphold
have obviously no relation to the question in hand.[42]

Further efforts of Justice, later Chief Justice, White to sterilize Congress's power over
interstate commerce in the interest of "dual
federalism" and State Rights will be noted in
subsequent chapters.

And meantime the same cause had received
another literary ally in Mr. Parmalee Prentice,
whose work *The Federal Power over Carriers
and Corporations* was brought out in 1907,
apropos of certain of President Theodore
Roosevelt's proposals for the regulation of the
railroads and of industrial corporations en-

[40] *ibid.*, 176-7.
[41] 236 U.S. 216 (1915).
[42] *ibid.*, 222.

gaging in interstate commerce. Pertinent passages from this volume follow:

From the foregoing review, it appears that the right to engage in commerce is derived from the States and that though Congress is given a power of regulation, it was nevertheless intended that the right itself should be beyond any governmental invasion—an element of personal liberty which the States could not deny nor the United States impair.

It is obvious, however, that there is a difference in the nature of Federal powers over foreign, Indian and interstate commerce. . . .

In foreign relations the general government stands in the place of and represents every State for every national purpose. It may exercise its control over foreign commerce to retaliate upon an unfriendly nation, or injure an enemy; to influence international negotiations, or to avoid being drawn into unnecessary quarrels. An embargo of foreign commerce may, therefore, be proper, for the Federal Government, if compelled to grant or to continue its authority and protection in all conditions, could not control its own foreign relations.

As to commerce among the States, no such considerations arise. Here the subject is presented solely as between the individual, and State and Federal governments. It is not affected by international considerations, nor does the United States in these relations take the place of or represent, a State or State laws.

This difference between the powers of regulation over foreign and over interstate commerce has been recognized from the beginning. . . .

In regulating foreign commerce, the national power is limited by the equal power of the foreign government. In interstate commerce, Congress is limited by the constitutional rights of citizens. . . . Members of the Supreme Court when the subject has arisen, have called attention to the difference. . . .

Mr. Prentice at this point quotes the extract given above from the *dissenting* opinion in the Lottery Case, at the same time neglecting to mention that it is a dissenting opinion from which he is quoting. He then concludes:

Transportation from State to State of legitimate articles of commerce cannot be forbidden. Congress is authorized to regulate, not to destroy, commerce among the States.[43]

The Madison-Tucker-Fuller-White-Prentice doctrine became the doctrine of the Court in the first Child Labor Case in 1918. This is not to say that the full Madisonian thesis was ratified by the Court in this decision. The Court had prior to this rendered too many decisions of contrary import to make such ratification possible. For all that, the decision in *Hammer v. Dagenhart* did ratify the Madisonian thesis sufficiently to render it a most formidable obstacle in the way of effective regulation by Congress of interstate business in furtherance of what Congress may judge to be the general welfare. And the same decision transfers the ultimate discretion in the use of the interstate commerce power from Congress to the Supreme Court. All of which will appear in clearer light in the course of the ensuing chapters.

[43] Prentice, P., *The Federal Power over Carriers and Corporations* (1907), 48-51.

With two recent judicial utterances reflecting the Court's continued approval of the Madisonian differentiation between Congress's power in the two principal fields of commercial activity, this chapter may be brought to a close. The first is the following passage from Justice Sutherland's opinion in *Atlantic Cleaners and Dyers v. United States*:[44]

It is not unusual for the same word to be used with different meanings in the same act, and there is no rule of statutory construction which precludes the courts from giving the word the meaning which the legislature intended it should have in each instance. *Louisville & N. R. Co. v. Gaines* (C. C.) 2 Flipp. 621, 3 Fed. 266, 277, 278. Thus, for example, the meaning of the word "legislature," used several times in the federal Constitution, differs according to the connection in which it is employed, depending upon the character of the function which that body in each instance is called upon to exercise. *Smiley v. Holm*, 285 U.S. 355, ante, 795, 52 S. Ct. 397, decided April 11, 1932. And, again in the Constitution, the power to regulate commerce is conferred by the same words of the commerce clause with respect both to foreign commerce and interstate commerce. Yet the power when exercised in respect of foreign commerce, may be broader than when exercised as to interstate commerce. In the regulation of foreign commerce an embargo is admissible; but it reasonably cannot be thought that, in respect of legitimate and unobjectional articles, an embargo would be admissible as a regulation of interstate commerce, since the primary purpose of the clause in respect of the latter was to secure freedom of commercial intercourse among the States. See *Groves v. Slaughter*, 15

[44] 286 U.S. 427 (1932).

Pet. 449, 505; *Southern S. S. Co. v. Portwardens*, 6 Wall. 31, 32, 33; *Buttfield v. Stranahan*, 192 U.S. 470, 492. Compare *Russell Motor Car Co. v. United States*, 261 U.S. 514, 520, 521.[45]

This invocation by Justice Sutherland of "the rules of statutory construction" provides a fitting close to the judicial argument for Proposition I. It is, of course, as Justice Sutherland says, well recognized that a word which recurs in a document may not always sustain throughout the document the same meaning, although the legal *presumption* is that it does so. But that a word should have *two* quite different meanings in a single short sentence in which it occurs but *once*, is certainly a novelty to the science of hermeneutics and probably to that of linguistics as well.

The latest judicial utterance bearing on the subject comprises the following passages from the opinion of the Court in *University of Illinois v. United States*.[46] Said Chief Justice Hughes:

The Congress may determine what articles may be imported into this country and the terms upon which importation is permitted. No one can be said to have a vested right to carry on foreign commerce with the United States. *Buttfield v. Stranahan, supra; The Abby Dodge*, 223 U.S. 166, 176, 177; *Brolan v. United States*, 236 U.S. 216, 218, 219; *Weber v. Freed*, 239 U.S. 325, 329, 330. If the Congress saw fit to lay an embargo or to prohibit altogether the importation of specified

[45] *ibid.*, 433-4.
[46] 289 U.S. 48 (1933).

articles, as the Congress may (*The Brigantine William*, 2 Hall's Amer. L. J., 255; Fed. Cas. No. 16,700; *Gibbons v. Ogden, supra*, pp. 192, 193; *Brolan v. United States, supra; Weber v. Freed, supra; Atlantic Cleaners & Dyers v. United States*, 286 U.S. 427, 434) no State by virtue of any interest of its own would be entitled to override the restriction. The principle of duality in our system of government does not touch the authority of the Congress in the regulation of foreign commerce. . . .

In international relations and with respect to foreign intercourse and trade the people of the United States act through a single government with unified and adequate national power. There is thus no violation of the principle which petitioner invokes, for there is no encroachment on the power of the State as none exists with respect to the subject over which the federal power has been exerted. To permit the States and their instrumentalities to import commodities for their own use, regardless of the requirements imposed by the Congress, would undermine, if not destroy, the single control which it was one of the dominant purposes of the Constitution to create. It is for the Congress to decide to what extent, if at all, the States and their instrumentalities shall be relieved of the payment of duties on imported articles.[47]

It should be added that neither of the dicta just quoted, so far as they go to sustain Proposition I, was essential to the decision of the question before the Court. The only case in which the Madisonian distinction between Congress's power in the two principal commercial fields may be said to have played a vital part, at least until very recently, is

[47] *ibid.*, 57-9.

Hammer v. Dagenhart and even there it is not mentioned. Even so, it must be conceded that had the majority of the Court in that case regarded Congress's power over interstate commerce to be of the same scope and degree as its power over foreign commerce, its decision must have sustained the legislation there involved.

CHAPTER THREE

PROPOSITION II

PROPOSITION II

That the power to regulate commerce among the States does not comprise the power to prohibit it.

1. *EARLY VIEWS ON PROHIBITIONS AND MONOPOLIES*

IT is conceded that the States originally had the power to prohibit commerce with one another; and it is clear that the words of the constitutional clause, given simply their literal force and effect, transfer the previous power of the States over interstate commerce to the national legislative organ.

As to the scope of State regulative power prior to the Constitution, the following items furnish illustrative evidence:

(1) The vast number of State tariff acts prior to 1789.[1]

(2) On July 13, 1785, Congress considered in committee of the whole a proposal to regulate "the trade of the States, as well with foreign nations as with each other. . . . Provided . . . that the legislative power of the several States shall not be restrained from pro-

---

[1] David Walter Brown, *The Commercial Power of Congress* (1910), 19-27. This was an excellent work in its day, and should have nullified the effect of the Tucker and Prentice volumes, but seems in fact to have passed almost unregarded.

hibiting the importation or exportation of any species of goods or commodities whatever."[2]

(3) In August, 1786, a subcommittee of the Grand Committee of the Continental Congress, of which Charles Pinckney was a member, recommended a 14th article to the Articles of Confederation: "The United States in congress assembled shall have the sole and exclusive power of regulating the trade of the several States, as well with foreign nations as with each other. . . . Provided . . . that the legislative power of the States shall not be restrained from laying embargoes in times of scarcity. . . ."[3]

(4) Already, June 16, 1785, Monroe had written Jefferson, in commendation of a proposal of like nature to the above: "The political economy of each State is entirely within its own direction. . . . The effect of this report would be to put the commercial economy of every State entirely under the hands of the Union."[4]

The point does not require elaboration. The restraints imposed by the States upon one another's commerce were one of the immediate causes of the Convention of 1787.

And that the National Government would, under the Constitution, take over this restrictive power upon commerce among the States,

[2] Elliot, *Debates* (1861), I, 111.
[3] Brown, *op. cit.*, 41-2.
[4] *ibid.*, 45-6.

was perceived from the first. The following items are evidence on this point.

In the Convention, Madison records, "Mr. Wilson mentioned. . . . As to mercantile monopolies, they are already included in the power to regulate trade. Col. Mason was for limiting the power to the single case of canals. He was afraid of monopolies of every sort which he did not think were by any means implied by the Constitution as supposed by Mr. Wilson."[5]

Soon afterward, however, Mason came to the conclusion that Congress would have the power to grant monopolies in the commercial field; and this was one of the reasons which both he and Gerry gave for refusing to sign the Constitution and for opposing its adoption.[6]

Also, it should be noted that five States, Massachusetts, New Hampshire, New York, North Carolina and Rhode Island, all proposed amendments to the Constitution to forbid Congress creating commercial monopolies.[7]

Pursuing the same thought, an able writer in Massachusetts, styling himself "Agrippa," opposed adoption of the Constitution partly on the ground that Congress would possess such large powers over interstate commerce. He declared that Congress would have "the

[5] Farrand, *Records*, II, 616.
[6] *ibid.*, 633, 640.
[7] Brown, 146.

unlimited right to create monopolies" and grant "exclusive charters." Comparing Congress's power to that formerly claimed by the British Parliament over the intercolonial trade, he demanded an amendment to the Constitution which would take from Congress the right to regulate intercourse among the States.[8]

On the other hand, Dawes, a member of the Massachusetts Ratifying Convention, demanded an act excluding foreigners from the coastwise trade,[9] and in 1793 Congress met this demand in large part by enacting the statute which was sustained in *Gibbons v. Ogden*.

The broad premises upon which the decision in *Gibbons v. Ogden* was based were pointed out above in discussing Proposition I, but the following items from Webster's argument in the case are also pertinent in connection with the present topic: "Congress," said he, "is to give the rule—to establish the system—to exercise the control over the subject." Such exercises of power should be left to Congress. "Of this character he considered monopolies of trade or navigation; embargoes; the system of navigation laws." But "all useful regulation does not consist in restraint; and that which Congress sees fit to leave free is a part of its regulation, as much as the

[8] P. L. Ford (Ed.), *Essays on the Constitution*, 70-1, 97, 98, 118.
[9] Elliot, II, 57-8.

rest."[10] And he later added, "The granting of monopolies of this kind is always referred to the power over commerce," in which connection he cited the power of the British monarch.[11]

In short, the word "regulate" connotes *restraint* primarily; and this also was the view of Madison, as late as 1832, with reference to the power to regulate foreign commerce.[12]

2. *THE LESSON OF THE JEFFERSONIAN EMBARGO*

The idea that the power to regulate commerce does not include the power to prohibit it was first invented, *not in relation to Congress's power over interstate commerce, but in relation to its power over foreign commerce*, that branch of commerce, in other words, over which Congress's power of regulation is conceded today to be unlimited. The immediate occasion for this brilliant contribution to the art of constitutional interpretation was Jefferson's Embargo, but even in this connection it was late in appearing.

Thus, no objection on constitutional grounds was raised to the embargo of 1794 or to the later non-intercourse acts, nor to the original Jeffersonian embargo. The constitutional argument seems to have been hatched

[10] 9 Wheat. 1, 15-18.
[11] *ibid.*, 26.
[12] *Letters and Other Writings*, IV, 236.

in the fertile if erratic brain of John Randolph. He raised three objections. First, that the embargo was not limited as to time; that it violated the ban on export taxes; and that it delegated legislative power. Later speakers brought forward other objections to the act of 1809 for enforcing the embargo, to the effect that this measure violated rights of persons under the Bill of Rights. A few speakers to the later measure enlarged upon Randolph's objection that the embargo was to run indefinitely. They denied that the people intended to give Congress power "to prohibit commerce altogether," or asserted that the embargo power was not a branch of the commercial power but only of the war power. These arguments were strongly contested by defenders of the embargo and the act for enforcing the embargo was carried in both Houses by a large majority.[13]

A picturesque presentation of the constitutional argument, so far as it rested on the alleged distinction between prohibition and regulation, is the following:

MR. TAGGERT: In the eighth section of the first article of the Constitution, power is given to Congress to regulate commerce with foreign nations, between the several States, and with the Indian tribes. In the ninth section of the same article, Congress is expressly prohibited from laying a duty or tax upon the exports of

[13] See *Annals of Congress*, 10th Cong., 1st Sess., II, cc. 2087, 2090-1, 2095-6, 2114-15, 2124-7, 2129-30, 2145-7, 2225; 2nd Sess., cc. 251, 260-76, 288, 291-5, 870-1, 1005, 1011.

any State. And in the tenth amendment to that instrument, which has been ratified by the several States so as to become part of the Constitution, we find it stated, that the powers not delegated to the United States by the Constitution, nor prohibited by it to the States, are reserved by it, to the States respectively, or to the people. Congress may regulate commerce. If a power to interdict or annihilate commerce is a necessary appendage to the power of regulation, then, it must be confessed that Congress possesses that power. But, Mr. Speaker, supposing you should hand your watch to a proper artisan, in order to have it regulated, and he should dash it to pieces in your presence, would you call this regulating? I believe not. But might he not plead in his justification the construction put upon the power vested in Congress, by the Constitution, to regulate commerce? Supposing the affair did not proceed that length. Supposing he only removed the mainspring, and laid it aside, to consume with filth and rust, and told you that he would replace it again, and reduce all the wheels into order, so as to make it an excellent watch, on the happening of certain events entirely without his own control; would that be considered as a legitimate appendage to his power of regulating? I believe not. But could he not prove that he possessed this right, by the construction put upon the Constitution of the United States? Congress is expressly prohibited by the Constitution from laying a duty upon exports, to the amount of so much as one single cent. Can it be supposed that the same instrument containing that prohibition should, upon any principles of fair construction, authorize the total interdiction of exports? Supposing that an express article for the purpose of empowering Congress to interdict all foreign commerce, say for one, two, or three years, or permanently, had been agitated in the Convention which framed the Constitution; can it be supposed that that body tremblingly alive to all encroachments, either upon personal liberty or State rights, would have acceded to such an article? No, it would have been spurned with contempt, as containing, not the mere germ, but the very quintessence of despotism; and no idea was, I trust, then entertained by what far-fetched construction, a justification of such a measure would be attempted hereafter. What would be thought of an interdict upon agriculture? Would any person suppose that Congress possess legitimate powers to say to the inhabitants of any one district, you shall hereafter abstain, either permanently or during the pleasure of the Government, from plowing, sowing, reaping, &c? Is there any person who would attempt to justify the issuing of such a mandate on Constitutional grounds? I believe not. But commercial pursuits are equally lawful and laudable with agriculture, and the merchant is equally entitled to the fostering care of Government with the man who cultivates the soil. Nay, were it not for a market for surplus produce, and for the reception of such articles in return as are furnished by the merchant, where would be the prosperity of agriculture itself? The farmer would be deprived of the most powerful stimulus to industry. A controversy between the merchant and the agriculturist would, pretty much, resemble the controversy in the fable between the hands and the feet on one side, and the belly on the other. Withdraw the support from the latter and all the members will languish.[14]

The same line of reasoning was developed in the judicial forum in the case of the *William*, and was rejected by a United States district court, in the following words:

JUDGE DAVIS: It is contended, that Congress is not invested with powers, by the Constitution, to enact laws, so general and so unlimited, relative to commer-

[14] *ibid.*, 870-1 (December 1808).

cial intercourse with foreign nations, as those now under consideration. It is well understood, that the depressed state of American commerce, and complete experience of the inefficacy of State regulations, to apply a remedy, were among the great, procuring causes of the federal Constitution. It was manifest, that other objects, of equal importance, were exclusively proper for national jurisdiction; and that under national management and control, alone, could they be advantageously and efficaciously conducted. The Constitution specifies those objects. A national sovereignty is created. Not an unlimited sovereignty, but a sovereignty, as to the objects surrendered and specified, limited only by the qualifications and restrictions, expressed in the Constitution. Commerce is one of those objects. The care, protection, management and control, of this great national concern, is, in my opinion, vested by the Constitution, in the Congress of the United States; and their power is sovereign, relative to commercial intercourse, qualified by the limitations and restrictions, expressed in that instrument, and by the treaty-making power of the President and Senate. "Congress shall have power to regulate commerce with foreign nations, and among the several States, and with the Indian tribes." Such is the declaration in the Constitution. Stress has been laid, in the argument, on the word "regulate," as implying, in itself, a limitation. Power to regulate, it is said, cannot be understood to give a power to annihilate. To this it may be replied, that the acts under consideration, though of very ample extent, do not operate as a prohibition of all foreign commerce. It will be admitted that partial prohibitions are authorized by the expression; and how shall the degree, or extent, of the prohibition be adjusted, but by the discretion of the national government, to whom the subject appears to be committed? Besides, if we insist on the exact and critical meaning of the word "regulate," we must, to be consistent, be equally critical with the substantial term, "commerce." The term does not necessarily include shipping or navigation; much less does it include the fisheries. Yet it never has been contended, that they are not the proper objects of national regulation; and several acts of Congress have been made respecting them. It may be replied, that these are incidents to commerce, and intimately connected with it; and that Congress, in legislating respecting them, are under the authority, given them by the Constitution, to make all laws necessary and proper, for carrying into execution the enumerated powers. Let this be admitted; and are they not at liberty, also, to consider the present prohibitory system, as necessary and proper to an eventual beneficial regulation? I say nothing of the policy of the expedient. It is not within my province. But, on the abstract question of constitutional power, I see nothing to prohibit or restrain the measure. . . .

If it be admitted that national regulations relative to commerce, may apply it as an instrument, and are not necessarily confined to its direct aid and advancement, the sphere of legislative discretion is, of course, more widely extended, and, in time of war, or of great impending peril, it must take a still more expanded range. Congress has power to declare war. It, of course, has power to prepare for war; and the time, the manner, and the measure, in the application of constitutional means, seem to be left to its wisdom and discretion. . . . Must we understand the nation as saying to their government: "We look to you for protection and security, against all foreign aggressions. For this purpose, we give you the control of commerce; but, you shall always limit the time, during which this instrument is to be used. This shield of defense you may, on emergent occasions, employ; but you shall always announce to us and to the world, the moment when it shall drop from your hands." . . .

Under the confederation, Congress could have no agency relative to foreign commerce, but through the medium of treaties; and, by the ninth article, it was stipulated, that no treaty of commerce should be made, whereby the legislative power of the respective States, should be restrained, from imposing such imposts and duties on foreigners, as their own people were subjected to, "or from prohibiting the exportation of any species of goods or commodities whatsoever." Here we find an express reservation to the State legislatures of the power to pass prohibitory commercial laws, and, as respects exportations, without any limitations. Some of them exercised this power. In Massachusetts, it was carried to considerable extent, with marked determination, but to no sensible good effect. One of the prohibitory acts of that State, passed in 1786, was for the express "encouragement of the agriculture and manufactures in our own country." The other, which was a counteracting law, had no definite limitation, but was to continue in force, until Congress should be vested with competent powers, and should have passed an ordinance for the regulation of the commerce of the States. Unless Congress, by the Constitution, possess the power in question, it still exists in the State legislatures—but this has never been claimed or pretended, since the adoption of the federal Constitution; and the exercise of such a power by the States, would be manifestly inconsistent with the power, vested by the people in Congress, "to regulate commerce." Hence I infer, that the power, reserved to the States by the Articles of Confederation, is surrendered to Congress, by the Constitution; unless we suppose, that, by some strange process, it has been merged or extinguished, and now exists no where.[15]

Obviously, much of this opinion would be equally applicable to sustain a Congressional

[15] 28 Fed. Cas. (No. 16,700), 614, 620-3.

prohibition of a sweeping nature upon commerce among the States.

3. PRO-SLAVERY AND THE COMMERCE CLAUSE

The transfer of the above argument against the Jeffersonian Embargo upon foreign commerce to the field of the interstate commerce power was effected by the defenders of slavery, who feared that Congress might put a ban upon the interstate slave trade. The time and place of the transfer mentioned can be given definitely. It occurred in 1841, in connection with the argument before the Supreme Court of the Mississippi Slave Question.[16] The immediate issue was whether a certain clause of the Mississippi constitution should be interpreted as prohibiting *ex proprio vigore* the introduction into that State of slaves from other States, and whether if it did so, it encroached upon Congress's power to regulate commerce among the States. The discussion took a wide range, but the decision avoided the question with which this volume is concerned, by holding that the clause of the Mississippi constitution which was involved was inoperative of itself and had never been put into effect. Here we shall give attention only to such parts of argument of counsel or

[16] *Groves v. Slaughter*, 15 Pet. 449.

opinions of the judges as bear directly upon Proposition II, above.

MR. CLAY: The last question in the case is, whether the provision of the Constitution of the United States, which gives to Congress, exclusively, the right to regulate commerce between the States, is opposed by the Constitution of Mississippi. The argument for the plaintiffs in error, is on the abolition side of the question. The counsel for the defendant sustain the opposite principle. The object of prohibition [provision?] in the Constitution of the United States is to regulate commerce; to sustain it, not to annihilate it. It is conservative. Regulation implies continued existence—life, not death; preservation, not annihilation; the unobstructed flow of the stream, not to check or dry up its waters. But the object of the abolitionists is to prevent the exercise of this commerce. This is a violation of the right of Congress under the Constitution.

The right of the States to regulate the condition of slaves within their borders, is not denied. It is fully admitted. Every State may, by its laws, fix the character and condition of slaves. The right of Congress to regulate commerce between the different States, which may extend to the regulation of the transportation of slaves from one State to another, as merchandize, does not affect these rights of the States. But to deny the introduction of slaves, as merchandize, into a State, from another State, is an interference with the Constitution of the United States. After their introduction, they are under the laws of the States. Nor is the power, given by the Constitution of the United States, to regulate commerce, one in which the States may participate. It is exclusive. It is essentially so: and its existence in this form is most important to the slaveholding States.[17]

[17] *ibid.*, 488-9.

Mr. Robert J. Walker took a very different attitude, treating with merited sarcasm a position which is a close approximation to that of the Court today.

But again, this power to regulate commerce is an active power, a power "to prescribe the rules" by which that commerce may be conducted, and to enforce those rules; but here it is said, no rule can be prescribed by Congress on this subject, or enforced, no law can be passed by Congress, to regulate this trade, but nevertheless, that the States cannot regulate nor prohibit this trade, because Congress has the exclusive power. This is a strange contradiction, Congress cannot legislate as to this case, although it may as to all other commerce among the States; but notwithstanding, the State law is void, because the power is vested in Congress. The power is vested in Congress, but nevertheless, it has no power to pass any law on the subject. But who is it that has the power? The Constitution says, Congress shall have the power to regulate; and yet it is contended, Congress have no power to regulate this trade, but nevertheless, the State law is void, in the absence of all power in Congress to legislate on the subject. It is rendered, then, a judicial power, to be put in force by this Court, and not by legislation; and yet have the judiciary any power to regulate commerce among the States? It is a sullen, dog-in-the-manger, power, that can neither act itself, nor permit action by any other authority.[18]

As already remarked, the constitutional issue was not decided. Two of the Justices, however, incorporated in their opinions observations bearing upon it.

Justice McLean, an anti-slavery man, seems

[18] *ibid*. (Appendix), 660.

to have been greatly impressed by a suggestion of Walker's, that if slaves were regarded
by the Constitution as property, and hence as
subjects of commerce, Congress could force
the interstate slave trade upon the "free"
States. He said:

Under the power to regulate foreign commerce, Congress impose duties on importations, give drawbacks,
pass embargo and non-intercourse laws, and make all
other regulations necessary to navigation, to the safety
of passengers, and the protection of property. Here is
an ample range, extending to the remotest seas where
the commercial enterprise of our citizens shall go, for
the exercise of this power. The power to regulate commerce among the several States is given in the same
section, and in the same language. But it does not
follow, that the power may be exercised to the same
extent.

The transportation of slaves from a foreign country,
before the abolition of that traffic, was subject to this
commercial power. This would seem to be admitted in
the Constitution, as it provides "the importation of
such persons as any of the States, now existing, shall
think proper to admit, shall not be prohibited by Congress, prior to the year 1808: but a tax or duty, may
be imposed on such importation, not exceeding ten
dollars for each person." An exception to a rule is said
to prove the existence of the rule; and this exception
to the exercise of the commercial power, may well be
considered as a clear recognition of the power in the
case stated. The United States are considered as a unit,
in all regulations of foreign commerce. But this cannot
be the case where the regulations are to operate among
the several States. The law must be equal and general
in its provisions. Congress cannot pass a non-intercourse law, as among the several States; nor impose an

embargo that shall affect only a part of them. Navigation, whether on the high seas, or in the coasting trade,
is a part of our commerce; and when extended beyond
the limits of any State, is subject to the power of Congress. And as regards this intercourse, internal or foreign, it is immaterial, whether the cargo of the vessel
consists of passengers, or articles of commerce.

Can the transfer and sale of slaves from one State
to another, be regulated by Congress, under the commercial power? If a State may admit or prohibit slaves
at its discretion, this power must be in the State, and
not in Congress. . . .

The Constitution treats slaves as persons. . . .

And what can more unanswerably establish the doctrine, that a State may prohibit slavery, or, in its discretion, regulate it, without trenching upon the commercial power of Congress? The power over slavery
belongs to the States respectively. It is local in its
character, and in its effects; and the transfer or sale of
slaves cannot be separated from this power. . . .[19]

Justice Baldwin, on the other hand, gave a
new and striking form to Clay's suggestion
that Congress's power over commerce among
the States was "conservative." This he applied
to mean, *conservative of property* dealt in in
trade between the States; and he bolstered
this adaptation of Clay's idea by reference to
the due process clause of Amendment V. His
opinion thus anticipates in a very interesting
way Chief Justice Taney's similar argument in
the Dred Scott Case respecting Congress's
power to govern territories of the United

[19] *ibid.*, 505-8.

States.[20] The pertinent portion of his opinion follows:

The conclusion, therefore, is inevitable, that slaves were embraced by the Constitution, as the subjects of commerce and commercial regulations, to the same extent as other goods, wares or merchandize. On no other construction can the ninth section of the first article be taken as an exception to the third clause of the eighth section: and when so taken, there is no escape from the construction declared in the opinion of the Court, in *Gibbons v. Ogden*. Besides, if the power to regulate commerce does not include the power to prohibit the importation of slaves into the United States, after 1808, when the exception in the ninth section of the first article does not operate, such power is not to be found in any other grant by the Constitution. . . .

Slaves, then, being articles of commerce with foreign nations, up to 1808, and until their importation was prohibited by Congress, they were also articles of commerce among the several States, which recognized them as property capable of being transferred from hand to hand as chattels. Whether they should be so held or not, or what should be the extent of the right of property in the owner of a slave, depended on the law of each State. . . .

As each State has plenary power to legislate on this subject, its laws are the test of what is property; if they recognize slaves as the property of those who hold them, they become the subjects of commerce between the States which so recognize them, and the traffic in them may be regulated by Congress, as the traffic in other articles; but no further. Being property, by the law of any State, the owners are protected from any violations of the rights of property by Congress, under the Fifth Amendment of the Constitution. . . . It

[20] *ibid.*, 514-16. 19 How. 393, 450 (1857).

follows, likewise, that any power of Congress over the subject is, as has been well expressed by one of the plaintiffs' counsel, conservative in its character, for the purpose of protecting the property of the citizens of the United States, which is a lawful subject of commerce among the States, from any State law which affects to prohibit its transmission for sale from one State to another, through a third or more States.

Nine years later, in *United States v. Marigold*,[21] the Court asserted the power of Congress to levy embargoes and lay prohibitions upon foreign commerce, in unqualified terms. Said Justice Daniel, speaking for the Court:

Congress are, by the Constitution, vested with the power to regulate commerce with foreign nations; and however, at periods of high excitement, an application of the terms "to regulate commerce" such as would embrace absolute prohibition may have been questioned, yet, since the passage of the embargo and non-intercourse laws, and the repeated judicial sanctions those statutes have received, it can scarcely, at this day, be open to doubt that every subject falling within the legitimate sphere of commercial regulation may be partially or wholly excluded, when either measure shall be demanded by the safety or by the important interests of the entire nation. Such exclusion cannot be limited to particular classes or descriptions of commercial subjects; it may embrace manufactures, bullion, coin, or any other thing. The power once conceded, it may operate on any and every subject of commerce to which the legislative discretion may apply it.[22]

[21] 9 How. 559.
[22] *ibid.*, 566-7.

In recent years the question of the power of Congress to prohibit commerce among the States has become involved with another issue, to which we now turn. In general, Congress's prohibitions upon designated branches of trade among the States were sustained on very broad grounds, until we come to the first Child Labor Case, *Hammer v. Dagenhart*. Here the Court called an abrupt halt upon the previously prevailing tendency and doctrine, and by a five-to-four decision extended to employers of child labor the benefits of the doctrines which had been adumbrated in *Groves v. Slaughter* for the benefit of the owners of slave labor.

PROPOSITION III

PROPOSITION III

That while Congress has power to restrain commerce among the States for the benefit of such commerce, this power is not available for the promotion of the general welfare in other respects.

1. *THE ISSUE DEFINED*

THE above proposition requires clarification. When is an act of Congress to be deemed a *restraint* on commerce? Does the term imply that the act in question diminishes the total *amount* of commerce, or rather that it diminishes the *freedom of judgment* of those who are engaged in the commercial activity which the act seeks to control? Generally it would seem that the former result is assumed to flow automatically from the latter, though with one exception. The Sherman Act is today interpreted as designed not to *restrain* commerce, but to *free* it from restraint by individuals who might wish to *monopolize* it. By closing to business judgment the road to monopoly, the act is presumed to preserve and enlarge commercial activity.

Reference should also be made to the effort, for example, by Mr. Prentice in his work, to discuss the Interstate Commerce Act of 1887 as a regulation merely of "*the instrumentalities of commerce,*" the idea being apparently that with this label affixed to it, the act ceases to be a precedent for restrictive legislation by Congress. Fortunately, there is no need to debate this and similar contentions, as Proposition III has been dealt with by the Court free from such refinements or "idea-isms" more than once.

Two other matters, however, must be mentioned here by way of anticipating what is to be said in subsequent chapters. It was seen in Chapter I that one of the principal arguments against conceding to Congress the right to restrain commerce among the States in order to promote a larger general welfare is the contention that Congress would be thus enabled to invade the reserved powers of the States, and especially what is termed their "police power," which is defined as the power to promote the public health, safety, morals, and general welfare. This phase of the general question of Congress's power over interstate commerce is dealt with in detail in the next chapter and hence is only touched upon incidentally in the present chapter.

Again, the mere statement of Proposition III serves to raise the vastly important question whether the Court is entitled to make the supposed purpose of Congress in passing a law a test of the constitutionality thereof. On the answer returned to this question hinges the relation of judicial review to legislative sovereignty, than which no more fundamental constitutional issue can be imagined. This phase of our general problem is reserved for Chapter VII below. In the present chapter the issue raised by Proposition III is discussed on its merits, and may be phrased thus: Is Congress entitled by a correct theory of the Constitution, and without regard to the inherent limits of judicial review, to place restraints upon commerce among the States in order to forward its own views of national welfare?

2. *NATIONAL SOVEREIGNTY TRIUMPHANT*

The Preamble of the Constitution reads as follows:

We, the People of the United States, in order to form a more perfect Union, establish Justice, insure domestic tranquillity, provide for the common defense, promote the general welfare, and secure the blessings of liberty to ourselves and our posterity, do ordain and establish this Constitution for the United States of America.

While the Preamble is not, of course, a grant of power, it nevertheless states the objects which the Constitution and the government set up by it are expected to foster, and these objects are not, obviously, to be comprehended completely in any idea of commercial prosperity however broad.

The earliest judicial evaluation of the contention that commerce may be restrained only for its own benefit is contained in the following passage from the opinion of the United States District Court in 1808, in the case of the *William*, which was quoted extensively under Proposition II:

Further, the power to regulate commerce is not to be confined to the adoption of measures, exclusively beneficial to commerce itself, or tending to its advancement; but, in our national system, as in all modern sovereignties, it is also to be considered as an instrument for other purposes of general policy and interest. The mode of its management is a consideration of great delicacy and importance; but, the national right, or power, under the Constitution, to adapt regulations of commerce to other purposes, than the mere advancement of commerce, appears to me unquestionable. Great Britain is styled, eminently, a commercial nation; but commerce is, in fact, a subordinate branch of her national policy, compared with other objects. . . . Maritime and naval strength is the great object of national solicitude; the grand and ultimate objects are the defense and security of the country. The situation of the United States, in ordinary times, might render legislative interferences, relative to commerce, less necessary; but the capacity and power of managing and directing it, for the advancement of great national purposes, seems an important ingredient of sovereignty. It was perceived, that, under the power of regulating commerce, Congress would be authorized to abridge it, in favor of the great principles of humanity and justice. Hence the introduction of a clause, in the Constitution, so framed as to interdict a prohibition of the slave trade, until 1808. Massachusetts and New York proposed a stipulation, that should prevent the erection of commercial companies, with exclusive advantages. Virginia and North Carolina suggested an amendment, that "no navigation law, or law regulating commerce, should be passed, without the consent

of two-thirds of the members present, in both Houses."
These proposed amendments were not adopted, but
they manifest the public conceptions, at the time, of
the extent of the powers of Congress, relative to commerce.[1]

Apparently Proposition III was first fore-
shadowed in the Supreme Court in 1892,
over a hundred years after the institution of
government under the Constitution. That
year Mr. James Coolidge Carter, as counsel
for Rapier in the case of *In re Rapier*,[2] attacked the constitutionality of the Act of 1890
closing the mails to all publications advertising lotteries, in the following terms:

But we insist that Congress has no power to exclude
matter concerning lotteries from the mails on the
ground that the circulation of such matter would have
an immoral or injurious tendency. That this was its
real purpose has already been shown. In enacting that
statute it was not exercising the power of regulating
the mail service, for there was no relation between the
means employed and that end. The real power which
it attempted to exercise was to hamper and impede,
and, if possible, to destroy, the lottery business, in
order to protect the people of the United States from
the assumed demoralizing and dangerous tendency of
lotteries. Inasmuch as no one pretends that Congress
may pass a law directly suppressing lotteries on the
ground that they have an immoral tendency, or, indeed, on any ground whatever, the question is whether
it can pass a law, not directly suppressing them by declaring them to be crimes, but harassing and obstruct-
ing them by withdrawing from them facilities which

[1] 28 Fed. Cas. (No. 16,700), 604, 621.
[2] 143 U.S. 110.

are under its control for no other reason than that it
deems them crimes which it would suppress if it had
the power? This question must be promptly answered
in the negative, for the power thus attempted to be
exercised is a power to suppress lotteries and that alone.
No such power can be derived from any express language in the Constitution, nor by any just implication
from any language in it. More than this, the possession
of any such power by Congress is utterly inconsistent
with the whole theory of the Constitutional relations
between the general government and the States.
Against all such views we respectfully insist that where
Congress cannot by direct legislation pronounce a
business to be a crime and punish it as such, but that
power has been reserved to the States, it is not competent to Congress to determine it to be a crime, and
to deprive it of the benefit of the mails for the sole purpose of endeavoring to suppress it. What cannot be
done directly cannot be done indirectly. Cooley's
Constitutional Limitations, 208; *Taylor v. Commissioners
of Ross County*, 23 Ohio St. 22.

A plausible attempt may be made to retort upon us
the argument drawn from possible consequences. "Is
it true, then," it may be asked, "that the government
of the United States is placed in the singular attitude
that it cannot discharge its duty of maintaining a mail
service without extending the facilities which that service affords to criminals of every description to aid
them in the commission of crime? Cannot that government decline to become the principal instrumentality
in the circulation, for instance, of obscene books and
pictures, without an entire abrogation of its postal
service? Are the statutes passed for that purpose also
invalid?" Whatever force the argument thus suggested
may seem to have is more apparent than real. It is
founded upon a failure to notice fundamental distinctions in the nature of criminal offenses.

The grand and principal distinctions between right and wrong, between what is criminal and what is innocent (and we mean the practical and existing distinctions, and not absolute or theoretical ones), are not created by laws. . . .

When the government of the United States was formed, with legislative and judicial powers, it must have been assumed that those powers would be exercised in accordance with the rules of morality—those distinctions between right and wrong—which obtained universally in the societies over which it was to extend. But, on the other hand, political societies have the power to create new distinctions between right and wrong, and thus to declare practices before regarded as innocent, or indifferent, to be criminal offenses and to punish them as such. Every completely sovereign power is clothed with this function; but a government not completely sovereign may or may not have it. The charter of its powers must be scrutinized in order to ascertain how far its authority in this direction extends.

Turning to the division of powers made by our Constitution between the States and the general government, we find, as its most distinctive feature, that certain enumerated powers were awarded to the latter, and all others reserved to the former. And among the powers so reserved most certainly that of determining what new things should be declared and treated as criminal offenses against the good order of society was embraced, except so far as distinct powers of legislation upon particular subjects were conferred upon the general government.

There is, therefore, a well defined line which limits the extent to which the general government can act as a moral person, and regulate its powers so as to favor or disfavor particular acts of individuals in the States. That line is, in general, coincident with the boundary everywhere recognized as separating *mala prohibita* from *mala in se*.[3]

While this argument deals with Congress's postal powers, it is easily transferable—and was soon to be transferred— to the power over interstate commerce. It was Mr. Carter's desire to contend that Congress's power over the mails extended to the *maintenance and improvement of the mail service, and no further*; but he was forced to qualify this position by a concession to the decencies, and to that degree to weaken it. However, he compensated for this defect by bringing in a supplementary argument based on the reserved powers of the States—since these extend to the protection of the public morals, Congress's powers may not be constitutionally exerted except in a moral vacuum. In other words, *when the Constitution delegated certain powers to the National Government, that moment these same powers became confined to the protection and extension of the subject-matter with which they immediately deal, and hence were stricken from the list of governmental powers in this country which are available to promote the larger purposes of good government elsewhere throughout the world!*

Mr. Carter's argument was effectively answered by Assistant Attorney General Maury in the following words:

[3] *ibid.*, 116-19.

The whole system of the transportation of the mails is built upon the power to establish post-offices and post-roads. *Legal Tender Cases*, 12 Wall. 457, 537. In the somewhat inadequate language of the power, and in the studied reticence of the Constitution in regard to it, we find an invitation to Congress to use a wide discretion as to ways and means. Under this power Congress has established a comprehensive postal service, and enacted laws regulating it, one of which is section 3894 of the Revised Statutes, as amended by the Act of September 19, 1890, 26 Stat. 465, c. 908, which provides that no newspaper, circular, pamphlet, etc., containing any advertisement of any lottery shall be carried in the mail, or delivered by any postmaster or letter-carrier, and makes it a penal offense to deposit such newspaper or publication in the mails for the purpose of such transportation. Has Congress the power to make this an offense?

To determine this question we must look at the nature of the power. The test is laid down by Chief Justice Marshall: "Whenever the terms in which a power is granted to Congress, or the nature of the power, require that it should be exercised exclusively by Congress, the subject is as completely taken from the State legislatures, as if they had been expressly forbidden to act upon it." *Sturges v. Crowninshield*, 4 Wheat. 122, 193.

From the nature of this power, it is vested exclusively in Congress; for it belongs to a class, which, like the power to regulate commerce, to declare war, to establish a uniform rule of naturalization, and to establish uniform laws on the subject of bankruptcies, is as exclusively vested in the United States as if their exercise by the States had been forbidden. It follows, as a sequence of immense significance, that the States have denuded themselves of the power to prevent the introduction, by the mails, of things that endanger the morals or the health of their people.

Here, then, is an undoubted surrender by the States of a fragment of their police power; just as in *McCulloch v. Maryland*, 4 Wheat. 316, and *Brown v. Maryland*, 12 Wheat. 419, the States were held to have surrendered a fragment of the taxing power; and in *Leisy v. Hardin*, 135 U.S. 100, they were held to have lost a fragment of their police power.

It is equally clear that the police power which the States have thus surrendered has, by the Constitution, been devolved upon Congress. If it has not, then the Constitution has resulted in a failure of government in a vital particular (and what graver necessity is there for the existence of a power, than the prevention of the failure of government?), or on the other hand, each State possesses a power within itself, which, by its very nature, should be uniform throughout all the States.

The assertion that power resides nowhere to prevent the transportation of such matter in the mails is somewhat appalling. The treaty making power has been assumed to be broad enough to exclude such matter from foreign mails; certainly the power to establish post-offices and post-roads should be equally broad as to the interstate mails.

There is a broad ground on which we may rest the implication that the Federal Government has a police power over such subjects. No power in the Constitution can be exercised in such a way as to defeat any one or more of the five great purposes for which the Constitution was ordained, namely: (1) to form a more perfect union: (2) to establish justice: (3) to insure domestic tranquillity: (4) to provide for the common defense: (5) to promote the general welfare.

It is not contended that from each of these a substantive power can be evolved; but the whole instrument is subordinate to these leading objects. To establish a postal system without forbidding, under proper sanctions, its use for purposes hurtful to the morals of the people of the several States, would have been to endanger, instead of to promote, the general welfare. Not only so, it would have been to weaken the bonds of the Union, instead of making them more perfect, if Congress had not legislated in the way complained of. From this partial surrender of State police power, and the duty of Congress to promote the general welfare, it follows by necessary implication, that Congress is clothed with all the police power over the mails that the several States would have had if the surrender had not been made.

This places Congress under an imperative duty to keep out of the mails everything that the representatives of the people in the several States, and of the States themselves, in Congress assembled, may properly exclude by a lawful use of police power. In *McCulloch's Case* the power implied to establish a bank was on the ground of convenience. Here, however, the power is absolutely necessary, to prevent a failure of government, the endangering of the general welfare and the weakening of the bonds of the Union itself. It is no exaggeration to say that such grave consequences would flow from permitting the lottery people of Louisiana to traffic in lottery tickets through public mails entering States where that traffic is prohibited as criminal.

We all know the disintegrating effect on the Union of the irritations growing out of slavery. Similar disintegrating forces would be the result of allowing the prostitution of the mails to the Louisiana lottery. The people of the several States would be driven to exasperation by the impunity thus given to the lottery in defiance of their laws. With the mail at its service, the lottery could defy the police power of the States. Is there not, then, a direct connection between the law in question and the power "to establish post-offices and post-roads"? it being well established that what is necessarily implied in the Constitution is as much a part of it as what is expressed in it. . . .

The necessity for such a power has driven the other side to a concession which is a virtual surrender of the argument: that a lottery is not a *malum in se*, but that it is *malum quia prohibitum*, and that the police power of Congress is restricted to matters *mala in se*.

This gives up the case—not only because it cannot rest on such fanciful distinctions, but also because lotteries are clearly *mala in se*. *Phelan v. Virginia, ubi supra*.

Such an argument is an anachronism, even in Louisiana, whose legislature has from time to time denounced lotteries as crimes to be severely punished, making it "the duty of the presiding judge of every court of criminal jurisdiction in this State, especially to charge every grand jury to inquire into all violations of the laws against lotteries, and against the unlawful selling of tickets in lotteries." It is an anachronism, because it regards lotteries from the standpoint from which they were regarded when the Constitution was formed.[4]

But the crucial battle over Proposition III was waged in the famous Lottery Case of 1902,[5] in which the question was the constitutionality of the Act of 1895, entitled "An Act for the suppression of lottery traffic through national and interstate commerce and the postal service." The case was thrice argued and the act was finally sustained by a five-to-four decision. Every phase of the issue raised by Proposition III was covered either by counsel or by the Justices speaking for the two wings of the Court.

[4] *ibid.*, 126-8.
[5] 188 U.S. 321.

The following extracts from the brief of Mr. William D. Guthrie, who appeared against the act, are the pertinent ones:

1. The suppression of lotteries is not an exercise of any power committed to the Congress by the Constitution of the United States, and is, therefore, in contravention of article X of the amendments, which provides that "the powers not delegated to the United States by the Constitution, nor prohibited by it to the States, are reserved to the States respectively, or to the people."

2. The sending of lottery tickets or policy slips does not constitute or evidence any transaction belonging to interstate commerce and is not within the scope of the power of the National Government to regulate commerce among the States.

3. The power to regulate lotteries, and to permit or prohibit the sale of lottery tickets, is exclusively within the jurisdiction of the police power reserved to the States.

I. It cannot be reasonably doubted that the intention and purpose of Congress, in the legislation now before the Court, was to suppress lotteries. There is no necessity to resort to the proceedings in Congress in which this purpose was openly avowed, for it appears on the face of the act itself expressly in its title and impliedly in its natural and reasonable effect. *Holy Trinity Church v. United States*, 143 U.S. 457, 462; *Henderson v. Mayor of N.Y.*, 92 U.S. 259, 268; *United States v. Fox*, 95 U.S. 670, 672; *Minnesota v. Barber*, 136 U.S. 313, 320. Yet hitherto no one has asserted that Congress has power to suppress lotteries any more than it has power to suppress insurance or speculation or other business between residents of different States not relating to interstate commerce. The suppression of lotteries or of any other harmful business is essentially an exercise of the police power exclusively within the domain of and expressly reserved to the several States.

In re Rahrer, 140 U.S. 545, 554; *United States v. E. C. Knight Co.*, 156 U.S. 1, 13. . . .

Further, if the Constitution delegated to Congress the express power to prohibit interstate commerce, that grant would not confer the power to prohibit directly or indirectly what was not interstate commerce. If Congress may prohibit the transportation of diseased animals or infected goods or obscene literature, it is because they are essentially commercial in their nature, and hence they are dealing with subjects of commerce. Such prohibition may be necessary and proper in order to protect the instrumentalities of interstate commerce and to safeguard such commerce. But this would not sanction the prohibition of things not constituting commerce, any more than Congress could forbid a citizen to go from one State to another on any business he saw fit and whatever his purpose might be.

IV. In reply to the question in the government's brief why may not the prohibitive power exercised in respect of foreign nations be applied to interstate commerce, and to the question why the same prohibitive power exercised in regulating trade with the Indian tribes may not be applied to interstate commerce, it should be sufficient to answer that there is nowhere in the Constitution or any of the amendments thereto a reservation of police powers or of any power either to any foreign nation or to any Indian tribe, and, therefore, the power of Congress over commerce with both is exclusive and absolute. . . .

The whole power to regulate every form of relations and intercourse with foreign countries resides in the sovereign national power created by the Constitution of the United States; and every manner of intercourse in its broadest signification, whether commercial intercourse or otherwise, is to be regulated, permitted or prohibited by Congress alone.

The source and scope of this power to regulate international commerce are, in their very nature, essentially different from the source and scope of the power to regulate domestic commerce. In the case of international commerce, there is no limitation whatever upon the power of Congress and no implied or reserved power in the States. In the case of internal or interstate commerce, the only power Congress exercises is that expressly delegated. . . .

The power to regulate commerce among the several States, it is true, is given in the same section and in the same language as the power to regulate foreign or international commerce, but the scope of the power is not the same in both cases and may not be exercised to the same extent. The same terms in relation to separate subjects frequently differ in meaning and scope.[6]

For the act appeared Assistant Attorney General James M. Beck, from whose able brief the following excerpts are culled:

1. The proceedings of the Convention of 1787 clearly show that the purpose of the framers was to vest in the Federal Government control, not merely over traffic, but over all intercommunication between the colonies themselves, or either of them, and the outside world.

Profoundly as the framers differed in other respects, it is clear that the absolute power which each constituent State had theretofore had over its external relations, of whatsoever nature, and which was denominated by the comprehensive word "commerce," should pass to the Federal Government. No residuum was left in the States. The purpose clearly was to empower Congress "to legislate in all cases as to which the separate States are incompetent, or in which the harmony of the United States may be interrupted by the

[6] *ibid.*, 326-34.

exercise of individual legislation." 2 Madison Papers, 859.

To remedy these evils the Constitutional Convention of 1787 was called, and so clearly were all delegates agreed as to the wisdom of taking from the thirteen States all control over their external relations, whether intercolonial or foreign, that the clause of the Constitution which was designed to effectuate this (art. 1, sec. 1) was passed without a dissenting voice and with comparatively little debate. While they did not in this section define commerce, yet they threw a searchlight on their meaning in a subsequent section whose history clearly reveals their purposes. Art. 1, sec. 9.

The power, therefore, that was taken from the States and vested in the United States was the power of each constituent State over its external relations and in its transfer to the Federal Government it was in no respect diminished, except by certain express limitations in the Federal compact, such as the prohibition of any preference of the port of one State over the port of another State (art. 1, sec. 9, par. 6) and the prohibition of duties upon exports (art. 1, sec. 9, par. 5) and of clearance duties (art. 1, sec. 9, par. 6).

With these minor limitations the delegated power was as exhaustive and plenary as that which it was intended to supersede. The question, therefore, as to what commerce is under the Federal Constitution necessarily depends upon what commerce was regarded to be by the colonies prior to the formation of the Constitution. Commerce meant the intercourse or intercommunication of a colony with the other colonies and the rest of the world, either by the importation or exportation of goods or by the ingress or egress of individuals, and was not confined to mere traffic in purchasable commodities. . . .

4. That the power to prohibit is absolute, and the legislature is the final judge of the wisdom of its ex-

ercise, seems to be clearly established upon both principle and authority.

The most familiar exercise of the power to regulate commerce in the minds of the men who framed the Federal Constitution was, doubtless, the total or partial prohibition of traffic in particular articles. This was often accomplished by duties; and those duties, so far as they were laid for prohibition, total or partial, and not for revenue, were regarded as regulations of commerce. . . .

Apart from the history of the period and the utterances of contemporaneous writers, the Constitution itself affords the most convincing proof that the right to regulate included the right to prohibit.

If the power to regulate did not include the right to prohibit, all the heated discussion in the Constitutional Convention on the prohibition of the slave trade was a case of "much ado about nothing."

It cannot be contended that the power to prohibit the migration of freemen and the importation of slaves is referable to any other clause in the Constitution. The framers of the Constitution regarded it as inherent in the power to regulate trade, and the exception that such legislation should not be made prior to 1808 is the clearest possible statement that after that year the prohibitory regulation could be made under the commerce clause of the Constitution.

In the exercise of its power to regulate foreign commerce, Congress has never hesitated to prohibit commerce in any particular article, or even to stop foreign commerce altogether, either for a fixed period of time or indefinitely. A well known instance of partial prohibition is that of obscene literature, which has been part of our laws ever since the tariff act of August 30, 1842, ch. 270, sec. 28. To the latter class belong the well known non-importation and embargo laws of the period prior to the war of 1812. See *Gibbons v. Ogden*, 9

Wheat. 1, 192-3; 2 Story on the Constitution, secs. 1264, 1289, 1290.

Congress has the same power over interstate commerce as over commerce with the Indian tribes. The question whether, under its power to regulate commerce with the Indian tribes, it could exclude any selected article from such commerce as deleterious, came up for decision in *United States v. Holliday*, 3 Wall. 407, 416-18, and was decided in the affirmative in an opinion by Mr. Justice Miller. *United States v. Le Bris*, 12 U.S. 278; *Sarlls v. United States*, 152 U.S. 570; *United States v. Mayrand*, 154 U.S. 552.

If Congress can exclude obscene literature from foreign commerce, why not from interstate commerce also; and if it can exclude obscene literature, why can it not exclude lottery tickets? If it can exclude spirituous liquors from commerce with the Indian tribes, why not from interstate commerce also; and if it can exclude spirituous liquors, why can it not exclude lottery tickets?

The principle has in effect already been decided by this Court. States have undertaken in the interests of the public health to exclude importations of a certain kind from other States, and their legislation has been held by this Court to be unconstitutional. *Railroad Co. v. Husen*, 95 U.S. 465; *Minnesota v. Barber*, 136 U.S. 313; *Brimmer v. Rebman*, 136 U.S. 78; *Voight v. Wright*, 141 U.S. 62. These laws were not held to be void, because they in effect levied taxes upon imports; for it is well settled that the word "imports" in the Constitution refers only to articles brought in from foreign countries. *License Cases*, 5 How. 504, 623; *Woodruff v. Parham*, 8 Wall. 123; *Brown v. Houston*, 114 U.S. 622, 628; *Coe v. Errol*, 116 U.S. 517, 526; *Pittsburg Co. v. Louisiana*, 156 U.S. 590, 600.

The laws were held void because they were regulations of commerce. But the Constitution does not expressly prohibit States from regulating commerce. It merely gives the power of regulation to Congress. Whenever, therefore, this Court has held a State law void as being a regulation of commerce, it has impliedly held that a law to the same effect could constitutionally be passed by Congress; that is, so far as Congress is not restrained by some express prohibition.

The legislative history of the United States gives many instances of prohibitory regulations of trade, none of which, to my knowledge, has ever been declared unconstitutional. Reference has already been made to the embargo acts and the prohibitions of trade with the Indians. The exclusion of aliens has already been discussed, and the identity of foreign and interstate commerce established by decisions of this Court.

5. *In re Rahrer*, 140 U.S. 545, evidences very strongly the power of Congress to prohibit interstate trade. The act of August 8, 1890, was passed by Congress with the full knowledge that in certain States of the Union the manufacture and sale of a recognized article of commerce was absolutely prohibited.

Disregarding the mere form of words, and looking to the substance of this act, in connection with State legislation, it was a virtual prohibition of transportation to that State. It is obvious that the power to pass such a law could not depend in any wise upon the State statute, but must be inherent in Congress, and therefore an absolute prohibition of transportation would have been valid if there had been no State statute. This Court held the virtual prohibition of the transportation of liquors to certain States a valid exercise of constitutional power. . . .

Steam and electricity have woven the American people into a closeness of life of which the framers of the Constitution never dreamed, and the necessity for Federal police regulations as to any matter within the Federal sphere of power becomes increasingly apparent. The constitutionality of arbitrary prohibitions can be discussed when such a case arises, and as yet no such case has arisen, but a reasonable and proper prohibition of immoral or unsafe trade through the channels of interstate commerce is a police power which belongs to the Republic as the sovereign authority over interstate trade. Such police power must exist somewhere as to interstate trade. It cannot be nonexistent. Obviously it does not exist in the States; therefore it must exist in the Federal Government, and there is nothing in the legislative or judicial history of the country that in any manner gainsays this conclusion.[7]

Is the power of Congress over interstate commerce that of a government which is sovereign within its delegated field, or is it a specially devised power intended to be used merely for the benefit of commerce? And if it is the latter, what has become of the power which belonged to the several States over intercourse with one another prior to the adoption of the Constitution? In other words, does the Constitution by a grant of power to Congress create a twilight zone in which neither Congress nor the States may act except to promote commerce? These are the principal points which this debate between Mr. Carter and Mr. Beck served to raise.

In the main, the opinion of the Court, delivered by Justice Harlan, ratified the Government's argument. The act was sustained on the broad ground that Congress was empowered to prohibit commerce in an article, dealing in which was not protected by the due

[7] *ibid.*, 335-44.

process clause of the Fifth Amendment, in order both to prevent the pollution of commerce and also to combat a widespread evil. The relevant portions of the opinion follow:

We have said that the carrying from State to State of lottery tickets constitutes interstate commerce, and that the regulation of such commerce is within the power of Congress under the Constitution. Are we prepared to say that a provision which is, in effect, a *prohibition* of the carriage of such articles from State to State is not a fit or appropriate mode for the *regulation* of that particular kind of commerce? If lottery traffic, carried on through interstate commerce, is a matter of which Congress may take cognizance and over which its power may be exerted, can it be possible that it must tolerate the traffic, and simply regulate the manner in which it may be carried on? Or may not Congress, for the protection of the people of all the States, and under the power to regulate interstate commerce, devise such means, within the scope of the Constitution, and not prohibited by it, as will drive that traffic out of commerce among the States? . . .

If a State, when considering legislation for the suppression of lotteries within its own limits, may properly take into view the evils that inhere in the raising of money, in that mode, why may not Congress, invested with the power to regulate commerce among the several States, provide that such commerce shall not be polluted by the carrying of lottery tickets from one State to another? In this connection it must not be forgotten that the power of Congress to regulate commerce among the States is plenary, is complete in itself, and is subject to no limitations except such as may be found in the Constitution. What provision in that instrument can be regarded as limiting the exercise of the power granted? What clause can be cited which, in any degree, countenances the suggestion that one may, of right, carry or cause to be carried from one State to another that which will harm the public morals? We cannot think of any clause of that instrument that could possibly be invoked by those who assert their right to send lottery tickets from State to State except the one providing that no person shall be deprived of his liberty without due process of law. We have said that the liberty protected by the Constitution embraces the right to be free in the enjoyment of one's faculties; "to be free to use them in all lawful ways; to live and work where he will; to earn his livelihood by any lawful calling; to pursue any livelihood or avocation, and for that purpose to enter into all contracts that may be proper." *Allgeyer v. Louisiana*, 165 U.S. 578, 589. But surely it will not be said to be a part of any one's liberty, as recognized by the supreme law of the land, that he shall be allowed to introduce into commerce among the States an element that will be confessedly injurious to the public morals.

If it be said that the Act of 1895 is inconsistent with the Tenth Amendment, reserving to the States respectively or to the people the powers not delegated to the United States, the answer is that the power to regulate commerce among the States has been expressly delegated to Congress.

Besides, Congress, by that act, does not assume to interfere with traffic or commerce in lottery tickets carried on exclusively within the limits of any State, but has in view only commerce of that kind among the several States. It has not assumed to interfere with the completely internal affairs of any State, and has only legislated in respect of a matter which concerns the people of the United States. As a State may, for the purpose of guarding the morals of its own people, forbid all sales of lottery tickets within its limits, so Congress, for the purpose of guarding the people of the United States against the "widespread pestilence of lotteries" and to protect the commerce which concerns all the States, may prohibit the carrying of lottery tickets from one State to another. In legislating upon the subject of the traffic in lottery tickets, as carried on through interstate commerce, Congress only supplemented the action of those States—perhaps all of them—which, for the protection of the public morals, prohibit the drawing of lotteries, as well as the sale or circulation of lottery tickets, within their respective limits. It said, in effect, that it would not permit the declared policy of the States, which sought to protect their people against the mischiefs of the lottery business, to be overthrown or disregarded by the agency of interstate commerce. We should hesitate long before adjudging that an evil of such appalling character, carried on through interstate commerce, cannot be met and crushed by the only power competent to that end. We say competent to that end, because Congress alone has the power to occupy, by legislation, the whole field of interstate commerce. What was said by this Court upon a former occasion may well be here repeated: "The framers of the Constitution never intended that the legislative power of the Nation should find itself incapable of disposing of a subject matter specifically committed to its charge." *In re Rahrer*, 140 U.S. 545, 562. If the carrying of lottery tickets from one State to another be interstate commerce, and if Congress is of opinion that an effective regulation for the suppression of lotteries, carried on through such commerce, is to make it a criminal offense to cause lottery tickets to be carried from one State to another, we know of no authority in the Courts to hold that the means thus devised are not appropriate and necessary to protect the country at large against a species of interstate commerce which, although in general use and somewhat favored in both national and State legislation in the early history of the country, has grown into disrepute and has become offensive to the entire people of the

Nation. It is a kind of traffic which no one can be entitled to pursue as of right. . . .

It is said, however, that if, in order to suppress lotteries carried on through interstate commerce, Congress may exclude lottery tickets from such commerce, that principle leads necessarily to the conclusion that Congress may arbitrarily exclude from commerce among the States any article, commodity or thing, of whatever kind or nature, or however useful or valuable, which it may choose, no matter with what motive, to declare shall not be carried from one State to another. It will be time enough to consider the constitutionality of such legislation when we must do so. The present case does not require the Court to declare the full extent of the power that Congress may exercise in the regulation of commerce among the States. We may, however, repeat, in this connection, what the Court has heretofore said, that the power of Congress to regulate commerce among the States, although plenary, cannot be deemed arbitrary, since it is subject to such limitations or restrictions as are prescribed by the Constitution. This power, therefore, may not be exercised so as to infringe rights secured or protected by that instrument. It would not be difficult to imagine legislation that would be justly liable to such an objection as that stated, and be hostile to the objects for the accomplishment of which Congress was invested with the general power to regulate commerce among the several States. But, as often said, the possible abuse of a power is not an argument against its existence. There is probably no governmental power that may not be exerted to the injury of the public. If what is done by Congress is manifestly in excess of the powers granted to it, then upon the Courts will rest the duty of adjudging that its action is neither legal nor binding upon the people. But if what Congress does is within the limits of its power, and is simply unwise or injurious, the remedy is that suggested by Chief Justice Marshall in *Gibbons v. Ogden*, when he said: "The wisdom and the discretion of Congress, their identity with the people, and the influence which their constituents possess at elections, are, in this, as in many other instances, as that, for example, of declaring war, the sole restraints on which they have relied, to secure them from its abuse. They are the restraints on which the people must often rely solely, in all representative governments."[8]

It will be observed that the Court relied largely on the conception of the commerce power set forth by Chief Justice Marshall in *Gibbons v. Ogden*, with however, one important qualification. *Throughout Justice Harlan assumes that while Congress's power over interstate commerce is not limited by the reserved powers of the States, it is limited by the protection which the Fifth Amendment—that is to say, the due process of law clause thereof—extends to rights of person and property.* The same idea recurs in later cases, as we shall note.

On the other hand, the minority opinion, by Chief Justice Fuller, owes much to Mr. John Randolph Tucker's work. The following excerpts are apposite:

The naked question is whether the prohibition by Congress of the carriage of lottery tickets from one State to another by means other than the mails is within the powers vested in that body by the Constitution of the United States. That the purpose of Congress in this enactment was the suppression of lotteries can-

[8] *ibid.*, 355-63.

not reasonably be denied. That purpose is avowed in the title of the act, and is its natural and reasonable effect, and by that its validity must be tested. *Henderson v. Mayor*, &c., 92 U.S. 259, 268; *Minnesota v. Barber*, 136 U.S. 313, 320.

The power of the State to impose restraints and burdens on persons and property in conservation and promotion of the public health, good order and prosperity is a power originally and always belonging to the States, not surrendered by them to the General Government nor directly restrained by the Constitution of the United States, and essentially exclusive, and the suppression of lotteries as a harmful business falls within this power commonly called of police. *Douglas v. Kentucky*, 168 U.S. 488.

It is urged, however, that because Congress is empowered to regulate commerce between the several States, it, therefore, may suppress lotteries by prohibiting the carriage of lottery matter. Congress may indeed make all laws necessary and proper for carrying the powers granted to it into execution, and doubtless an act prohibiting the carriage of lottery matter would be necessary and proper to the execution of a power to suppress lotteries; but that power belongs to the States and not to Congress. To hold that Congress has general police power would be to hold that it may accomplish objects not entrusted to the General Government, and to defeat the operation of the Tenth Amendment, declaring that: "The powers not delegated to the United States by the Constitution, nor prohibited by it to the States, are reserved to the States respectively, or to the people." . . .

The Constitution gives no countenance to the theory that Congress is vested with the full powers of the British Parliament, and that, although subject to constitutional limitations, it is the sole judge of their extent and application; and the decisions of this Court from the beginning have been to the contrary. . . .[9]

3. *PRESENT DOUBTFUL STATUS OF THE ISSUE*

But if the decision in the Lottery Case did not settle once and for all that Congress may prohibit commerce among the States in order to promote the general welfare, at least the decision a decade later in *Hoke v. United States*,[10] in which the White Slave Act of 1910 was sustained by a unanimous Court, would seem to have, especially when read in the light of the following paragraphs from Justice Mc-Kenna's opinion:

[9] *ibid.*, 364-73. A striking expression in Congress of the limited purpose theory of the national commercial power was that by Senator William M. Evarts of New York, in the course of the debate on the Interstate Commerce Act of 1887. He said:

"Whatever the effect of this bill as properly construed and as reasonably applied shall be upon commerce, it is the exercise of a power lodged in this Government, solely on the motive of commerce, not upon any other motive, not upon any other consideration than what either directly or by converting influence touches the regulation of commerce. . . . Nor, Mr. President, has the power of this Government the right or the duty of distributing population and either furthering or resisting operations that tend in that direction and with that effect. . . . What has happened has happened; what is to happen will happen; and if there is any line that is drawn between the powers of the Federal Government and the powers of the States it is this, that the domestic arrangements are to depend upon the determination of the State authority, and that this Government is neither a party nor is it a wisher in regard to the results and consequences that come out of the development of commerce or the changes of its methods except that this Government deals with this very subject itself of commerce in the interest of commerce." *Cong. Record*, XVIII, Pt. 1, pp. 603-4 (49th Cong., 2nd Sess.; Jan. 13, 1887).

[10] 227 U.S. 308 (1913).

Plaintiffs in error admit that the States may control the immoralities of its citizens. Indeed, this is their chief insistence, and they especially condemn the act under review as a subterfuge and an attempt to interfere with the police power of the States to regulate the morals of their citizens and assert that it is in consequence an invasion of the reserved powers of the States. There is unquestionably a control in the States over the morals of their citizens, and, it may be admitted, it extends to making prostitution a crime. It is a control, however, which can be exercised only within the jurisdiction of the States, but there is a domain which the States cannot reach and over which Congress alone has power; and if such power be exerted to control what the States cannot it is an argument for—not against—its legality. Its exertion does not encroach upon the jurisdiction of the States. We have cited examples; others may be adduced. The Pure Food and Drugs Act (June 30, 1906, 34 Stat. 768, c. 3915) is a conspicuous instance. In all of the instances a clash of national legislation with the power of the States was urged, and in all rejected.

Our dual form of government has its perplexities, State and Nation having different spheres of jurisdiction, as we have said, but it must be kept in mind that we are one people; and the powers reserved to the States and those conferred on the Nation are adapted to be exercised, whether independently or concurrently, to promote the general welfare, material and moral. This is the effect of the decisions, and surely if the facility of interstate transportation can be taken away from the demoralization of lotteries, the debasement of obscene literature, the contagion of diseased cattle or persons, the impurity of food and drugs, the like facility can be taken away from the systematic enticement to and the enslavement in prostitution and debauchery of women, and, more insistently, of girls.

This is the aim of the law expressed in broad generalization; and motives are made of determining consequence. Motives executed by actions may make it the concern of Government to exert its powers. Right purpose and fair trading need no restrictive regulation, but let them be transgressed and penalties and prohibitions must be applied. We may illustrate again by the Pure Food and Drugs Act. Let an article be debased by adulteration, let it be misrepresented by false branding, and Congress may exercise its prohibitive power. It may be that Congress could not prohibit the manufacture of the article in a State. It may be that Congress could not prohibit in all of its conditions its sale within a State. But Congress may prohibit its transportation between the States, and by that means defeat the motive and evils of its manufacture. . . .

The principle established by the cases is the simple one, when rid of confusing and distracting considerations, that Congress has power over transportation "among the several States"; that the power is complete in itself, and that Congress, as an incident to it, may adopt not only means necessary but convenient to its exercise, and the means may have the quality of police regulations.[11]

Yet five years later the Court, by a vote of 5 to 4, overturned the Child Labor Act of 1916, forbidding the transportation from one State to another of goods into the manufacture of which child labor had entered. That this result invoked Proposition III was in effect recognized by Chief Justice Taft, speaking for the Court in the Child Labor Tax Case.[12] The pas-

[11] ibid., 321-3 passim.
[12] Bailey v. Drexel Furniture Co., 259 U.S. 20 (1922).

sage in his opinion which is alluded to is the following:

The congressional power over interstate commerce is, within its proper scope, just as complete and unlimited as the congressional power to tax, and the legislative motive in its exercise is just as free from judicial suspicion and inquiry. Yet when Congress threatened to stop interstate commerce in ordinary and necessary commodities, unobjectionable as subjects of transportation, and to deny the same to the people of a State in order to coerce them into compliance with Congress's regulation of State concerns, the Court said this was not in fact regulation of interstate commerce, but rather that of State concerns and was invalid. So here the so-called tax is a penalty to coerce people of a State to act as Congress wishes them to act in respect of a matter completely the business of the State government under the Federal Constitution. This case requires as did the *Dagenhart Case* the application of the principle announced by Chief Justice Marshall in *McCulloch v. Maryland*, 4 Wheat. 316, 423, in a much quoted passage:

"Should Congress, in the execution of its powers, adopt measures which are prohibited by the Constitution; or should Congress, under the pretext of executing its powers, pass laws for the accomplishment of objects not intrusted to the government; it would become the painful duty of this tribunal, should a case requiring such a decision come before it, to say, that such an act was not the law of the land."[13]

In other words, while Congress would have power to keep child labor from harming commerce among the States, it is powerless to pre-

[13] *ibid.*, 39-40. The meaning of the passage quoted from Marshall's opinion is discussed at the outset of Chapter VII, pp. 215-21, *infra*.

vent commerce among the States from harming child labor!

In two recent cases which bear on Proposition III the spokesman for the Court was
Justice Roberts. These are *Railroad Retirement Board v. Alton R. Co.*,[14] and the current
case of *United States v. Butler*, in which the
A. A. A. was set aside. The latter decision can
be more instructively treated later, but the
Alton Case must be dealt with at this point as
illustrating admirably the limited purpose
theory of national power.

The act of Congress under review required
railway carriers to contribute to a pension
fund for superannuated employees. The Court,
five Justices to four, held the act void both as
violative of the due process clause of the Fifth
Amendment and as not falling within the
power to regulate interstate commerce. Said
Justice Roberts, on the latter point, which is
the one of interest here:

It has and can have no relation to the promotion of
efficiency, economy or safety by separating the unfit
from the industry. If these ends demand the elimination of aged employees, their retirement from the
service would suffice to accomplish the object. For
these purposes the prescription of a pension for those
dropped from service is wholly irrelevant. The petitioners, conscious of the truth of this statement,
endeavor to avoid its force by the argument that social
and humanitarian considerations demand the support
of the retired employee. They assert that it would be

[14] 295 U.S. 330 (1935).

unthinkable to retire a man without pension and add that attempted separation of retirement and pensions is unreal in any practical sense, since it would be impossible to require carriers to cast old workers aside without means of support. The supposed impossibility arises from a failure to distinguish Constitutional power from social desirability. The relation of retirement to safety and efficiency is distinct from the relation of a pension to the same ends, and the two relationships are not to be confused.

In final analysis, the petitioners' sole reliance is the thesis that efficiency depends upon morale, and morale in turn upon assurance of security for the worker's old age. . . .

The theory is that one who has an assurance against future dependency will do his work more cheerfully, and therefore more efficiently. The question at once presents itself whether the fostering of a contented mind on the part of an employee by legislation of this type, is in any just sense a regulation of interstate transportation. If that question be answered in the affirmative, obviously there is no limit to the field of so-called regulation. The catalogue of means and actions which might be imposed upon an employer in any business, tending to the satisfaction and comfort of his employees, seems endless. Provision for free medical attendance and nursing, for clothing, for food, for housing, for the education of children, and a hundred other matters, might with equal propriety be proposed as tending to relieve the employee of mental strain and worry. Can it fairly be said that the power of Congress to regulate interstate commerce extends to the prescription of any or all of these things? Is it not apparent that they are really and essentially related solely to the social welfare of the worker and therefore remote from any regulation of commerce as such? We think the answer is plain. These matters obviously lie outside the orbit of Congressional power. The answer of the petitioners is that not all such means of promoting contentment have such a close relation to interstate commerce as pensions. This is in truth no answer, for we must deal with the principle involved and not the means adopted. If contentment of the employee were an object for the attainment of which the regulatory power could be exerted, the courts could not question the wisdom of methods adopted for its advancement. . . .[15]

The Chief Justice, dissenting for himself and Justices Brandeis, Stone and Cardozo, summarized the purport of the Court's position as follows:

In substance, it is that the relation of the carriers and their employees is the subject of contract; that the contract prescribes the work and the compensation; and that a compulsory pension plan is an attempt for social ends to impose upon the relation non-contractual incidents in order to insure to employees protection in their old age. And this is said to lie outside the power of Congress in the government of interstate commerce. Congress may, indeed, it seems to be assumed, compel the elimination of aged employees. A retirement act for that purpose might be passed. But not a pension act. The government's power is conceived to be limited to a requirement that the railroads dismiss their superannuated employees, throwing them out helpless, without any reasonable provision for their protection.

The argument pays insufficient attention to the responsibilities which inhere in the carriers' enterprise. . . .[16]

He then continued:

The power of Congress to pass a compensation act to govern interstate carriers and their employees en-

---

[15] *ibid.*, 367-8.
[16] *ibid.*, 381-2.

gaged in interstate commerce does not seem to be questioned. . . .

What sound distinction, from a constitutional standpoint, is there between compelling reasonable compensation for those injured without any fault of the employer, and requiring a fair allowance for those who practically give their lives to the service and are incapacitated by the wear and tear of time, the attrition of the years? I perceive no constitutional ground upon which the one can be upheld and the other condemned.

The fundamental consideration which supports this type of legislation is that industry should take care of its human wastage, whether that is due to accident or age. That view cannot be dismissed as arbitrary or capricious. It is a reasoned conviction based upon abundant experience. The expression of that conviction in law is regulation. When expressed in the government of interstate carriers with respect to their employees likewise engaged in interstate commerce, it is a regulation of that commerce. As such, so far as the subject-matter is concerned, the commerce clause should be held applicable.[17]

The issue between the majority and the minority in this case, while arising in a comparatively narrow field, that of Congress's power to regulate the relations of interstate carriers to their employees, is the very issue presented by Proposition III. Justice Roberts says that Congressional legislation in this field must be justified by its tendency to promote efficient service on the part of the carriers; Chief Justice Hughes says that Congress may legislate to secure essential justice for the em-

[17] *ibid.*, 384.

ployees. He assumes, in other words, that Congress has the same power that any civilized legislature would claim in dealing with that particular subject.

As for Justice Roberts's fear of legislation requiring free medical service, and so on, it would seem from his own opinion, that the present Court at least would have no difficulty in dealing with such legislation on the basis of the due process clause, which is the *only* restraint available against similar legislation by the States.

Two years ago, in *Nebbia v. New York*,[18] Justice Roberts was also the spokesman for a closely divided Court. Sustaining the legislation there at bar, he said:

Thus has this Court from the early days affirmed that the power to promote the general welfare is inherent in government. Touching the matters committed to it by the Constitution, the United States possesses the power (*United States v. DeWitt*, 9 Wall. 41; *Gloucester Ferry Co. v. Pennsylvania*, 114 U.S. 196, 215) as do the States in their sovereign capacity touching all subjects jurisdiction of which is not surrendered to the Federal Government, as shown by the quotations above given. These correlative rights, that of the citizen to exercise exclusive dominion over property and freely to contract about his affairs, and that of the State to regulate the use of property and the conduct of business, are always in collision. No exercise of the private right can be imagined which will not in some respect, however slight, affect the public; no exercise of the legislative prerogative to regulate the conduct

[18] 291 U.S. 502 (1934).

of the citizen which will not to some extent abridge his liberty or affect his property. But subject only to constitutional restraint the private right must yield to the public need.

The Fifth Amendment, in the field of federal activity (*Addyston Pipe & Steel Co. v. United States*, 175 U.S. 211, 228-9), and the Fourteenth, as respects State action (*Barbier v. Connolly*, 113 U.S. 27, 31; *Chicago, B. & Q. R. Co. v. Drainage Comm'rs*, 200 U.S. 561, 592), do not prohibit governmental regulation for the public welfare. They merely condition the exertion of the admitted power, by securing that the end shall be accomplished by methods consistent with due process. And the guaranty of due process, as has often been held, demands only that the law shall not be unreasonable, arbitrary or capricious, and that the means selected shall have a real and substantial relation to the object sought to be attained. It results that a regulation valid for one sort of business, or in given circumstances, may be invalid for another sort, or for the same business under other circumstances, because the reasonableness of each regulation depends upon the relevant facts.[19]

The only restriction indicated here, as in the Lottery Case, to the use by Congress of its delegated powers to promote the general welfare is that the limitations of the Fifth Amendment should not be transcended.

Although both are by the same Justice, this opinion and that in the Alton Case clearly represent very different approaches to the problem raised by Proposition III.

[19] *ibid.*, 524-5.

PROPOSITION IV

PROPOSITION IV

That the reserved powers of the States constitute a limitation upon Congress's power to regulate commerce among the States and serve to withdraw certain matters from the jurisdiction of the latter power.

Some of the material already passed in review, particularly that set forth in discussions of Proposition III, bears upon the above proposition as well. Further material will now be reviewed.

1. *EARLY NATIONALISM*

THE pertinent provisions of the Constitution in this connection are the following:

The Congress shall have power . . . to regulate commerce with foreign nations and among the several States.[1]

To make all laws which shall be necessary and proper for carrying into execution the foregoing powers, and all other powers vested by this Constitution in the government of the United States, or in any department or officer thereof.[2]

This Constitution, and the laws of the United States which shall be made in pursuance thereof; and all treaties made, or which shall be made, under the authority of the United States, shall be the supreme law of the land; and the judges in every State shall be bound thereby, any thing in the Constitution or laws of any State to the contrary notwithstanding.[3]

[1] Art. I, sec. 8, cl. 3.
[2] *ibid.*, cl. 18.
[3] Art. VI, par. 2.

The powers not delegated to the United States by the Constitution, nor prohibited by it to the States, are reserved to the States respectively, or to the people.[4]

Some of the members of the Philadelphia Convention, Madison being of the number, appear to have believed at first that power should be conferred upon the new government in broadly descriptive terms, rather than by specific enumeration. Evidence of this is afforded by the Sixth Randolph Resolution, of May 29, 1787, which read as follows:

Resolved that each branch ought to possess the right of originating Acts; that the National Legislature ought to be impowered to enjoy the Legislative Rights vested in Congress by the Confederation and moreover to legislate in all cases to which the separate States are incompetent, or in which the harmony of the United States may be interrupted by the exercise of individual Legislation; to negative all laws passed by the several States, contravening in the opinion of the National Legislature the articles of Union; and to call forth the force of the Union agst. any member of the Union failing to fulfill its duty under the articles thereof.[5]

Later, however, a consensus of opinion developed that the proposed government should be one of *enumerated* powers, but *supreme* as to those powers, while conversely the States

[4] Amend. X.
[5] Farrand, I, 21. See also Madison's statement, May 31, that he had brought to the Convention "a strong bias in favor of" an enumeration of powers, but that his doubts of its feasibility had increased. *ibid.*, 53.

should be left "in possession of a considerable though subordinate jurisdiction."[6]

The following extract from Madison's notes for July 16 is significant:

The 6th Resol: in the Report from the Come. of the whole House . . . was now resumed. . . . "And moreover to legislate in all cases to which the separate States are incompetent; or in which the harmony of the U.S. may be interrupted by the exercise of individual legislation" (being read for a question).

Mr. Butler calls for some explanation of the extent of this power; particularly of the word *incompetent*. The vagueness of the terms rendered it impossible for any precise judgment to be formed.

Mr. Ghorum. The vagueness of the terms constitutes the propriety of them. We are now establishing general principles, to be extended hereafter into details which will be precise & explicit.[7]

In other words, the purpose of the above resolution was finally not to delegate indefinite powers to the new government, but to lay down a principle by which the Committee of Detail would be guided in selecting the subjects to which the jurisdiction of the proposed government ought to be extended. One of the subjects so selected was commerce among the States.

And with this understanding in mind, the following entries in the Journal of the Convention for July 17 take on their proper significance:

[6] *ibid.*, 355.
[7] *ibid.*, II, 17.

It was moved and seconded to postpone the considn of the second clause of the Sixth resolution reported from the Committee of the whole House in order to take up the following

"To make laws binding on the People of the United States in all cases which may concern the common interests of the Union: but not to interfere with the government of the individual States in any matters of internal police which respect the government of such States only, and wherein the general welfare of the United States is not concerned." which passed in the negative (Ayes—2; noes—8.) It was moved and seconded to alter the second clause of the 6th resolution so as to read as follows, namely

"and moreover to legislate in all cases for the general interests of the Union, and also in those to which the States are separately incompetent, or in which the harmony of the United States may be interrupted by the exercise of individual legislation

which passed in the affirmative (Ayes—6; noes —4.) . . .

It was moved and seconded to agree to the following resolution namely.

Resolved that the legislative acts of the United States made by virtue and in pursuance of the articles of Union and all Treaties made and ratified under the authority of the United States shall be the supreme law of the respective States as far as those acts or Treaties shall relate to the said States, or their Citizens and Inhabitants—and that the Judiciaries of the several States shall be bound thereby in their decisions, any thing in the respective laws of the individual States to the contrary notwithstanding. Which passed unanimously in the affirmative.[8]

In the Convention Madison had shown himself a strong advocate of national power, as

[8] *ibid.*, 21-2.

well as of the idea of curbing the States, over whose legislation he wished the national legislature to be given an unlimited veto. An instance of his disparagement of the States at this period is the following:

Some contend that States are sovereign, when in fact they are only political societies. There is a gradation of power over all societies, from the lowest corporation to the highest sovereign. The States never possessed the essential rights of sovereignty. These were always vested in Congress. Their voting, as States, in Congress, is no evidence of sovereignty. The State of Maryland voted by counties—did this make the counties sovereign? The States, at present, are only great corporations, having the power of making by-laws, and these are effectual only if they are not contradictory to the general confederation. The States ought to be placed under the control of the general government—at least as much so as they formerly were under the King and British Parliament. The arguments, I observe, have taken a different turn, and I hope may tend to convince all of the necessity of a strong energetic government, which would equally tend to give energy to, and protect the State governments.[9]

The Convention being over, Madison adopted a different tone, in advocating, both in the Virginia Ratifying Convention and in the *Federalist*, the adoption of the Constitution. In the Virginia Convention he said:

The powers of the general government relate to external objects, and are but few, but the powers in

[9] *ibid.*, I, 471-2. See also his statement, June 28, that the small States ought to promote "those principles and that form of government which will most approximate the States to the condition of counties." *ibid.*, 449.

the States relate to those great objects which immediately concern the prosperity of the people.[10]

Similarly, in the *Federalist* Madison sought to assure opponents of the Constitution that the jurisdiction of the proposed government extended "to certain enumerated objects only," and left "to the States a residuary and inviolable sovereignty over all other objects."[11]

On the other hand, when on June 8, 1789, Madison introduced into the first House of Representatives a series of amendments to the Constitution, in fulfillment of a pledge on the part of supporters of the Constitution while its adoption was pending, he softened a proposal from some of the States, which would have reserved to the States all powers not "expressly" delegated to the United States, by eliminating the word *expressly*.[12] Furthermore, while this amendment was pending he stated the following canon of constitutional interpretation in the course of the Congressional debate on Hamilton's Bank proposal:

[10] Elliot, *Debates* (1851), III, 259. Cf. Wilson's statement in the Philadelphia Convention: "The State Governments ought to be preserved—the freedom of the people and their good police depend on their existence in full vigor—but such a government can only answer local purposes." Farrand, I, 157. See also Dickinson's statement in his *Letters of Fabius*, written in support of the Constitution while its adoption was pending: "The authority of the whole must be coextensive with its interests . . . or else the whole would have interests without authority to manage them, a position which prejudice itself cannot digest." *Political Writings*, II, 97.

[11] No. 39; Lodge, Ed., 238.

[12] *Writings* (Hunt, Ed.), V, 380.

Interference with the power of the States was no constitutional criterion of the power of Congress. If the power was not given, Congress could not exercise it; if given, they might exercise it, although it should interfere with the laws, or even the Constitution of the States.[13]

These words also state the attitude of the Supreme Court of that date. The principal argument offered against the Court's accepting in 1792 jurisdiction of the case of *Chisholm v. Georgia*[14] was based on the supposed immunity of a "sovereign" State from being sued without its consent. This argument was brushed aside by Justice Wilson with the statement that "as to the purposes of the Union . . . Georgia was not a sovereign State."[15] Likewise, in *Ware v. Hylton*[16] a treaty of the United States was held to invalidate retroactively a law which the State of Virginia was admitted to have had the power to enact in the first instance. Said Justice Chase:

If doubts could exist before the establishment of the present national government, they must be entirely removed by the 6th article of the Constitution, which provides "That all treaties made, or which shall be made, under the authority of the United States, shall be the supreme law of the land; and the Judges in every State shall be bound thereby, anything in the Constitution, or laws, of any State to the contrary notwithstanding." There can be no limitation on the power

[13] *Annals of Cong.*, 1st Cong., 2nd and 3rd Sess. (1790-91), c. 1891.
[14] 2 Dall. 419.
[15] *ibid.*, 457.
[16] 3 Dall. 199 (1796).

of the people of the United States. By their authority the State Constitutions were made, and by their authority the Constitution of the United States was established; and they had the power to change or abolish the State Constitutions, or to make them yield to the general government, and to treaties made by their authority. A treaty cannot be the supreme law of the land, that is of all the United States, if any act of a State legislature can stand in its way. If the Constitution of a State (which is the fundamental law of the State, and paramount to its Legislature) must give way to a treaty, and fall before it; can it be questioned, whether the less power, an act of the State legislature, must not be prostrate? It is the declared will of the people of the United States that every treaty made, by the authority of the United States, shall be superior to the Constitution and laws of any individual State; and their will alone is to decide—If a law of a State, contrary to a treaty, is not void, but voidable only by a repeal, or nullification by a State legislature, this certain consequence follows, that the will of a small part of the United States may control or defeat the will of the whole. The people of America have been pleased to declare, that all treaties made before the establishment of the National Constitution, or laws of any of the States, contrary to a treaty, shall be disregarded.[17]

In both *McCulloch v. Maryland*[18] and in *Gibbons v. Ogden* counsel advanced the contention that when an act of Congress, came into conflict with an act passed by a State in exercise of its reserved powers, the two acts confronted each other on a basis of exact equality. Marshall rejected the argument by an emphatic assertion of the principle of national

[17] *ibid.*, 236.
[18] 4 Wheat. 316 (1819).

supremacy. His words in *McCulloch v. Maryland* were as follows:

If any one proposition could command the universal assent of mankind, we might expect it would be this— that the government of the Union, though limited in its powers, is supreme within its sphere of action. This would seem to result necessarily from its nature. It is the government of all; its powers are delegated by all; it represents all, and acts for all. Though any one State may be willing to control its operations, no State is willing to allow others to control them. The nation, on those subjects on which it can act, must necessarily bind its component parts. But this question is not left to mere reason: the people have in express terms, decided it, by saying "this Constitution, and the laws of the United States, which shall be made in pursuance thereof," "shall be the supreme law of the land," and by requiring that the members of the State legislatures, and the officers of the executive and judicial departments of the States, shall take the oath of fidelity to it.

The government of the United States, then though limited in its powers, is supreme; and its laws, when made in pursuance of the Constitution, form the supreme law of the land, "any thing in the Constitution or laws of any State to the contrary notwithstanding."[19]

The pertinent portions of his opinion in *Gibbons v. Ogden* were given in Chapter 1. As he there indicated, the fact that certain subject-matter falls under the control of the reserved powers of the States does not serve to put such subject-matter beyond the reach of

[19] *ibid.*, 405-6. It is interesting to note that counsel for the State in this case regarded the Tenth Amendment as "merely declaratory." *ibid.*, 374.

Congress's delegated powers. Nor was the interest of the States in preserving their accustomed powers conceded by Marshall to be a controlling consideration in the interpretation of the delegated powers of the United States, since the latter came, not from the States, but from the people, and comprised "an investment of power for the general advantage, in the hands of agents selected for that purpose, which power can never be exercised by the people themselves, but must be placed in the hands of agents, or lie dormant."[20] *National power was to be liberally construed and effectively implemented, regardless of the coexistence of State powers*—this was the Marshall system of constitutional interpretation.

2. *THE REVIVAL OF STATES RIGHTS*

Upon Marshall's death a new point of view emerged. This found clear expression for the first time in a Supreme Court opinion in *New York v. Miln*,[21] where was upheld a New York statute laying certain requirements upon captains of vessels entering New York harbor with aliens aboard. Speaking for the Court, Justice Barbour said:

There is, then, no collision between the law in question, and the acts of Congress just commented on; and therefore, if the State law were to be considered as

[20] 9 Wheat. 1, 189.
[21] 11 Pet. 102 (1837).

partaking of the nature of a commercial regulation; it would stand the test of the most rigid scrutiny, if tried by the standard laid down in the reasoning of the Court, quoted from the case of *Gibbons v. Ogden.*

But we do not place our opinion on this ground. We choose rather to plant ourselves on what we consider impregnable positions. They are these: That a State has the same undeniable and unlimited jurisdiction over all persons and things, within its territorial limits, as any foreign nation; where that jurisdiction is not surrendered or restrained by the Constitution of the United States. That, by virtue of this, it is not only the right, but the bounden and solemn duty of a State, to advance the safety, happiness and prosperity of its people, and to provide for its general welfare, by any and every act of legislation, which it may deem to be conducive to these ends; where the power over the particular subject, or the manner of its exercise is not surrendered or restrained, in the manner just stated. That all those powers which relate to merely municipal legislation, or what may, perhaps, more properly be called *internal police*, are not thus surrendered or restrained; and that, consequently, in relation to these, the authority of a State is complete, unqualified and exclusive.[22]

The thought here is that the police powers of the States constitute a reserve of *exclusive* powers, with the result that any subject-matter which falls within their jurisdiction is, *for that reason*, outside the scope of the delegated powers of the United States. In effect this sets the Tenth Amendment on its head by requiring that State power, or at any rate a *part* of it, be defined prior to the definition of national

[22] *ibid.*, 139.

power, and not vice versa. Nor does it appear
by what warrant the reserved powers of the
States may be divided into two classes, one of
which limits national power, while the other is
limited thereby. Yet to extend the doctrine of
the Barbour dictum to all the reserved powers
of the States would obviously render the supremacy clause *entirely* nugatory.

It is interesting to note that counsel defending the New York statute had not advanced
any such proposition as that voiced here by
Justice Barbour, but had contented themselves
with an endeavor to show that the New York
act did not conflict with any act of Congress
or any treaty. What is more, Justice Wayne,
who was one of the majority for whom Justice
Barbour professed to speak in the Miln Case,
declared from the bench a few years later that
he had never assented to Barbour's "impregnable positions," and strongly hinted that
they had been smuggled into the Court's
opinion after it had been approved by the
other Justices.[23]

Despite all which, when we turn to the
License Cases,[24] we find that the new doctrine
that there is a field of jurisdiction which is ex-

[23] 7 How. 429-37. "Indeed, it would be most extraordinary if the
case of *Gibbons v. Ogden* could be considered as having been
reversed by a single sentence in the opinion of *New York v. Miln*;
upon a point, too, not in any way involved in the certificate of the
division of opinion by which that case was brought to this court."
ibid., 436.
[24] 5 How. 504 (1847).

clusively reserved to the States and to which for that reason, Congress's power over interstate commerce cannot constitutionally extend, has undergone considerable advance. Some extracts from counsel's argument, pro and con, of the issues are given first. The States Rights position was stated by Mr. Davis, of counsel, in the following terms:

This authority [*New York v. Miln*] defines the great question of boundary between the sovereignties with an accuracy which cannot be mistaken, so far as regards police laws.

The powers not conceded or prohibited by the constitution remain in the States unchanged, unaltered, and unimpaired, and as fully in force as if no constitution had been made.

None of those powers which relate to municipal legislation or internal police have been surrendered or restrained, but are complete, unqualified, and exclusive. . . .

The inference is irresistible, that such powers are independent of and paramount to the Constitution of the United States, and therefore not subject to any supreme power of the Federal Government in cases of conflict. . . .

The pressure of this principle of supremacy was forced upon the States with such zeal, and the supposed cases of incompatibility became so frequent, that the exigencies of the times demanded a positive rule to the extent that it could be safely established.

The step was taken eleven years ago, and what inconvenience has been experienced? In what has the power of the United States been impaired or disturbed? Who has sensibly felt any change? Whose interests have not been well provided for, and safely protected? Much has been said, and sung by the theorists; but the laws have been well harmonized, and the public have been well satisfied.

In regard to constitutional principle, this case is decisive of the one under consideration, as it admits the authority of a State to maintain police regulations in regard to its internal affairs, whatever may be their effect or influence upon the laws of the United States. . . .

The course of reasoning pursued is intended to establish the following positions: . . .

3. That, if the right of a State to maintain police laws is complete and unqualified, there can be no constitutional conflict with the laws of the United States, as the power is absolute and supreme. . . .

4. That the United States having a right to regulate foreign commerce is bounded by the point where such commerce becomes internal, and cannot follow it for the purposes of regulation or control after it becomes subject to State authority, without usurping the constitutional power of the State.[25]

This argument was met by Messrs. Whipple and Ames, of opposing counsel, as follows:

They admitted that an act of a State, to come in conflict with the exclusive power of Congress to regulate foreign commerce, when not exercised, must of itself be an exercise of that power; but maintained, that any law pertaining to the mere police of a State might come in conflict with a commercial regulation of Congress; and, if it did, must, so far as it did, yield to the law of Congress, as the supreme law of the land, when passed in pursuance of the Constitution. They were not aware, until the doctrine had been boldly advanced by the counsel for Massachusetts, in the preceding case,—tried with this by order of the Court,— that it had been a "growing opinion," and still less, that by the decision of this Court in *New York v. Miln*,

[25] *ibid.*, 527-37.

11 Pet. 139, 141 it had become "the settled law" of
this court and of the land, that in all such cases of
conflict the rule of the Constitution was reversed, and
that the law of Congress became subject to the law of
the State, as to the supreme law of the land, and that
the clause of the Constitution asserting the supremacy
of the Constitution, and of the laws and treaties of the
United States made under it, applied only to the case
of concurrent powers; nor did they so understand that
case. They maintained that the doctrine thus announced was little short of absurdity, since it admitted
the supremacy of the law of Congress in the case of
concurrent powers,—in the exercise of which the governments of the States and the government of the
United States enjoyed, as it were, a joint empire, and
where, from the very fact that the powers were concurrent, they could never, in a constitutional sense, be
said to conflict, and so there was no room for the
supremacy in question,—and denied the supremacy
of the United States in the legitimate exercise of its
exclusive powers, making the United States the slave
of the States in its own exclusive dominions, under a
Constitution which declared, without limitation or
reserve, that its just power should be supreme, not only
over the laws, but even the Constitutions, of the States.
Upon this question they appealed from conservative
Massachusetts to democratic Virginia, and cited the
44th Paper of the *Federalist*, p. 183, Gideon's edition,
in which Mr. Madison, in commenting upon the clause
of the Constitution in question, concludes his defense
against the only objection that was made to it—that
it rendered the Constitution, laws, and treaties of the
United States supreme over the Constitutions of the
States—with this statement of the result if this
supremacy had not been given:—"In fine, the world
would have seen, for the first time, a system of government founded on an inversion of the fundamental
principles of all government; it would have seen the

authority of the whole society everywhere subordinate
to the authority of the parts; it would have seen a
monster, in which the head was under the direction of
the members." In this case, a supremacy over the
Constitution, laws, and treaties of the United States
was claimed for every, even the most petty, police law
of a State, or even a town or city, when that Constitution and those laws and treaties were made supreme
over the Constitution of the State by which, or under
the authority of which, the police law was passed.
They commented upon the case of *New York v. Miln*,
for the purpose of showing that the general language
there used by Mr. Justice Barbour in delivering the
opinion of the Court, from which the strange doctrine
in question had been inferred, should, according to the
rule in this respect laid down by Mr. Chief Justice
Marshall in *Cohens v. Virginia*, 6 Wheat. 399, be restrained to the case before the Court, which, by the
decision of the Court, involved no conflict of the powers
of the government of the State of New York with those
of the government of the United States, and, by the
illustrations given of the meaning of the language,
could be fairly applied only to cases where no conflict
existed. Upon this point, they cited also the opinions of
Mr. Chief Justice Taney, and of Mr. Justice McLean,
in the subsequent case of *Groves et al. v. Slaughter*, 15
Pet. 505, 509, members of the Court at the time the
opinion in *New York v. Miln* was delivered, and con-
curring in that opinion, for the purpose of showing that
they could not have understood the language in question in the sense contended for.

(Mr. Justice Wayne here declared his entire dissent
from the general opinions expressed in the language
in question, and even declared that he had no recollec-
tion that such language was in the opinion of the Court
in that case at the time it received his concurrence.)

They concluded upon this point, that if any persons
really held the doctrine in question, upon the supposi-

tion that it was necessary for the maintenance of
certain peculiar institutions of some of the States,
which, though guaranteed by the Constitution, were at
war with its whole spirit, as well as with the principles
of the Declaration of Independence, which the Constitution carried out as far as it could consistently with
the existing condition of the country, they were guilty
of a "blunder,"—in the opinion of a great but un-
principled politician, in such matters, always worse
than "a crime." The clauses in the Constitution
guaranteeing these institutions were an anomaly in it.
It was better, then, to treat those institutions and
every thing fairly relating to them as anomalous—to
be governed by peculiar rules—than, by converting
an anomaly into a general rule, to pervert the whole
spirit, and invert the whole order, of the Constitution,
and, by thus stripping the general government of all
its powers, deprive the States, and especially the
smaller States, of all the rights and protection guaranteed by the United States.[26]

There can be no doubt that Messrs. Whipple
and Ames's insinuation that the doctrine of
the Barbour dictum was based on "the sup-
position that it was necessary for the maintenance of certain peculiar institutions of some of
the States" was more than a shrewd guess. The
South had long since become convinced that
the safety of slavery lay in crying up State
power and crying down national power; and
particularly was the power of Congress over
interstate commerce regarded as a standing
menace, first, because it might be turned
against the interstate slave trade, and, sec-

[26] *ibid.*, 544-6.

ondly, because it might be used to foist free negroes upon the slave States, there to become potential instigators of servile revolt. Justice Barbour's "impregnable positions" were, in other words, a sop to the Southern Cerberus, or in the slang of that day, "a tub thrown to the great Southern whale." Yet this is not the entire story, by any means. "States Rights" had become, to a greater or less degree, the constitutional creed of the entire country even before Marshall's death, a fact which he recognized and deplored. In the following quotations from certain opinions of the Justices in the License and Passenger Cases, it will be observed that those of Justice McLean, an anti-slavery man, are as strongly assertive of the doctrine of exclusive State powers as are those from the Southern Justices.

From the individual opinions filed in the License Cases (there was no opinion of the Court), the following extracts are most apposite to our problem:

CHIEF JUSTICE TANEY: The Constitution of the United States declares that that Constitution, and the laws of the United States which shall be made in pursuance thereof, and all treaties made, or which shall be made, under the authority of the United States, shall be the supreme law of the land. It follows that a law of Congress regulating commerce with foreign nations, or among the several States, is the supreme law; and if the law of a State is in conflict with it, the law of Congress must prevail, and the State law cease to operate so far as it is repugnant to the law of the United States.

It is equally clear, that the power of Congress over this subject does not extend further than the regulation of commerce with foreign nations and among the several States; and that beyond these limits the States have never surrendered their power over trade and commerce, and may still exercise it, free from any controlling power on the part of the general government. Every State, therefore, may regulate its own internal traffic, according to its own judgment and upon its own views of the interest and well-being of its citizens. . . .

It is unquestionably no easy task to mark by a certain and definite line the division between foreign and domestic commerce, and to fix the precise point, in relation to every important article, where the paramount power of Congress terminates, and that of the State begins. The Constitution itself does not attempt to define these limits. They cannot be determined by the laws of Congress or the States, as neither can by its own legislation enlarge its own powers, or restrict those of the other. And as the Constitution itself does not draw the line, the question is necessarily one for judicial decision, and depending altogether upon the words of the Constitution.[27]

JUSTICE McLEAN: There may be a limitation on the exercise of sovereign powers, but that State is not sovereign which is subject to the will of another. This remark applies equally to the Federal and State governments. The Federal government is supreme within the scope of its delegated powers, and the State governments are equally supreme in the exercise of those powers not delegated by them nor inhibited to them. From this it is clear, that while these supreme functions are exercised by the Federal and State governments, within their respective limitations, they can never come in conflict. And when a conflict occurs, the in-

[27] ibid., 573-4.

quiry must necessarily be, which is the paramount law? And that must depend upon the supremacy of the power by which it was enacted. The Federal government is supreme in the exercise of powers delegated to it, but beyond this its acts are unconstitutional and void. So the acts of the States are void when they do that which is inhibited to them or exercise a power which they have exclusively delegated to the Federal government. . . .

The States, resting upon their original basis of sovereignty, subject only to the exceptions stated, exercise their powers over every thing connected with their social and internal condition. A State regulates its domestic commerce, contracts, the transmission of estates, real and personal, and acts upon all internal matters which relate to its moral and political welfare. Over these subjects the Federal government has no power. They appertain to the State sovereignty as exclusively as powers exclusively delegated appertain to the general government.[28]

JUSTICE DANIEL: This provision of the Constitution, it is to be feared, is sometimes applied or expounded without those qualifications which the character of the parties to that instrument, and its adaptation to the purposes for which it was created, necessarily imply. Every power delegated to the Federal government must be expounded in coincidence with a perfect right in the States to all that they have not delegated; in coincidence, too, with the possession of every power and right necessary for their existence and preservation; for it is impossible to believe that these ever were, in intention or in fact, ceded to the general government. Laws of the United States, in order to be binding, must be within the legitimate powers vested by the Constitution. Treaties, to be valid, must be made within the scope of the same powers; for there can be no "authority of the United States," save what is derived

[28] *ibid.*, 588.

mediately or immediately, and regularly and legitimately, from the Constitution. A treaty, no more than
an ordinary statute, can arbitrarily cede away any one
right of a State or of any citizen of a State. In cases of
alleged conflict between a law of the United States and
the Constitution, or between a law of a State and the
Constitution or a statute of the United States, this
Court must pronounce upon the validity of either law
with reference to the Constitution; but whether the
decision of the Court in such cases be itself binding or
otherwise must depend upon its conformity with, or
its warrant from, the Constitution. It cannot be correctly held, that a decision, merely because it be by
the Supreme Court, is to override alike the Constitution and the laws both of the States and of the United
States.[29]

The theory which pervades these opinions
is the one which was urged upon Chief Justice
Marshall by counsel in both *McCulloch v.
Maryland* and *Gibbons v. Ogden*, only to be
rejected by him on each occasion. It is the
theory of two mutually exclusive, recipro-
cally limiting fields of power, the governmental
occupants of which confront each other as
equals. It follows that when each field is
properly delimited there can be no overlapping
of authorities; "and," to quote Chief Justice
Taney, "as the Constitution itself does not
draw the line, the question is necessarily one
for judicial decision, and depending altogether
on the words of the Constitution"—although
it is admitted that these do "not draw the
line"! In short, for the principle of national

[29] *ibid.*, 613.

supremacy is substituted that of judicial supremacy. And in the Passenger Cases[30] two years later the same theory finds repeated expression. On that occasion the Chief Justice said:

And the first inquiry is, whether, under the Constitution of the United States, the Federal government has the power to compel the several States to receive, and suffer to remain in association with its citizens, every person or class of persons whom it may be the policy or pleasure of the United States to admit. In my judgment, this question lies at the foundation of the controversy in this case. . . .

I had supposed this question not now open to dispute. It was distinctly decided in *Holmes v. Jennison*, 14 Pet. 540; in *Groves v. Slaughter*, 15 Pet. 449; and in *Prigg v. The Commonwealth of Pennsylvania*, 16 Pet. 539.

If these cases are to stand, the right of the State is undoubted. And it is equally clear, that if it may remove from among its citizens any person or description of persons whom it regards as injurious to their welfare, it follows that it may meet them at the threshold and prevent them from entering. . . .

Neither can this be a concurrent power, and whether it belongs to the general or to the State government, the sovereignty which possesses the right must in its exercise be altogether independent of the other. If the United States have the power, then any legislation by the State in conflict with a treaty or act of Congress would be void. And if the States possess it, then any act on the subject by the general government, in conflict with the State law, would also be void, and this Court bound to disregard it. It must be paramount and absolute in the sovereignty which possess it. A con-

[30] 7 How. 283.

current and equal power in the United States and the States as to who should and who should not be permitted to reside in a State, would be a direct conflict of powers repugnant to each other, continually thwarting and defeating its exercise by either, and could result in nothing but disorder and confusion. . . .

I can, therefore, see no ground for the exercise of this power by the government of the United States or any of its tribunals. In my opinion, the clear, established, and safe rule is, that it is reserved to the several States, to be exercised by them according to their own sound discretion, and according to their own views of what their interest and safety require. It is a power of self-preservation, and was never intended to be surrendered.[31]

And this also is the purport of Justice Daniel's and Justice Woodbury's opinions in dissent; and even Justice McLean, while holding the State laws involved in this particular case to be void, again reflects the same general theory as to the relation of national to State power:

A concurrent power excludes the idea of a dependent power. The general government and a State exercise concurrent powers in taxing the people of the State. The objects of taxation may be the same, but the motives and policy of the tax are different, and the powers are distinct and independent. A concurrent power in two distinct sovereignties to regulate the same thing is as inconsistent in principle as it is impracticable in action. It involves a moral and physical impossibility. A joint action is not supposed, and two independent wills cannot do the same thing. The action of one, unless there be an arrangement, must necessarily precede the action of the other; and that which

[31] *ibid.*, 465-70.

is first, being competent, must establish the rule. If the powers be equal, as must be the case, both being sovereign, one may undo what the other does, and this must be the result of their action.

But the argument is, that a State acting in a subordinate capacity, wholly inconsistent with its sovereignty, may regulate foreign commerce until Congress shall act on the same subject; and that the State must then yield to the paramount authority. A jealousy of the Federal powers has often been expressed, and an apprehension entertained that they would impair the sovereignty of the States. But this argument degrades the States by making their legislation, to the extent stated, subject to the will of Congress. State powers do not rest upon this basis. Congress can in no respect restrict or enlarge State powers, though they may adopt a State law. State powers are at all times and under all circumstances exercised independently of the general government, and are never declared void or inoperative except when they transcend State jurisdiction. And on the same principle, the Federal authority is void when exercised beyond its constitutional limits. . . .

In giving the commercial power to Congress the States did not part with that power of self-preservation which must be inherent in every organized community. They may guard against the introduction of any thing which may corrupt the morals, or endanger the health or lives of their citizens. Quarantine or health laws have been passed by the States, and regulations of police for their protection and welfare.[32]

Justice Wayne's opinion, on the other hand, followed in general the lines of Marshall's opinion in *Gibbons v. Ogden*. "The sovereign powers of the United States," said he, could

[32] *ibid.*, 399-400.

not "be carried out by legislation without acting upon the territory and sovereignty of the
States"; and it was error to overlook "that a
part of the supreme police power of a nation"
was "identical . . . with its sovereignty over
commerce." But even he curtailed the logic
of his position in favor of slavery, as follows:

All the political sovereignty of the United States,
within the States, must be exercised according to the
subject-matter upon which it may be brought to bear,
and according to what was the actual condition of the
States in their domestic institutions when the Constitution was formed, until a State shall please to alter
them. The Constitution was formed by States in which
slavery existed, and was not likely to be relinquished,
and States in which slavery had been, but was abolish-
ed, or for the prospective abolition of which provision
had been made by law. The undisturbed continuance
of that difference between the States at that time,
unless as it might be changed by a State itself, was the
recognized condition in the Constitution for the
national Union. It has that, and can have no other,
foundation. . . .

That is a very narrow view of the Constitution which
supposes that any political sovereign right given by it
can be exercised, or was meant to be used, by the
United States in such a way as to dissolve, or even dis-
quiet, the fundamental organization of either of the
States. The Constitution is to be interpreted by what
was the condition of the parties to it when it was
formed, by their object and purpose in forming it, and
by the actual recognition in it of the dissimilar institutions of the States. The exercise of constitutional power
by the United States, or the consequences of its ex-

ercise, are not to be concluded by the summary logic of ifs and syllogisms.[33]

3. *MIXED TENDENCIES*

At this point we encounter a fact of great significance. Despite all this vast proliferation of States-Rightism in arguments of counsel and in opinions of individual Justices prior to the Civil War, the very dubious opinion of Justice Barbour in the Miln Case aside, the Proposition under investigation in this chapter *never received the sanction of an authoritative opinion of the Court until after the Civil War*. And meantime motivation of the Proposition had undergone a fundamental change. The peculiar anxieties of the "peculiar institution" had ceased to trouble either the Court or anybody else, while States Rights, *as such*, were still under the shadow cast upon them by the secession movement. At the same time, the extreme character of the Radical Republican Reconstruction program had aroused the fear

[33] *ibid.*, 422, 427, 428-9. Two brief extracts from arguments of counsel are of interest. Said Mr. D. B. Ogden: "In my view of the Constitution, it is idle to talk of an invasion of State rights as a reason for not giving a fair and just construction to it. The very thing the people intended when they adopted the Constitution of the United States was, that it should be the supreme law of the land, and that this Court should have the power of construing it in all doubtful cases." *ibid.*, 295. Mr. Van Buren, on the other side, commented on the commerce clause as follows: "The terms used are capable of indefinite extension in the hands of a skilful construer. Commerce, in an enlarged sense, covers nearly all the business relations of society. Every law that qualifies or affects its transactions or relations necessarily regulates it." *ibid.*, 368.

of moderates throughout the country that the States were to be blotted out and the Federal system replaced by an entirely centralized system. Lastly, the Court was conscious of still being under a cloud also, on account of the Dred Scott decision.

To this mixed situation, the statesmanship of the Court, headed by such outstanding personalities as Chase, Miller, Field and Bradley, proved on the whole adequate. Two ideas rescued from the late Taney régime furnished the basis of its achievement. One was the dual federalism embodied in Proposition IV. The other was the idea that *the Court was a body standing somewhat outside of and above both the National Government and the States for the purpose of umpiring between the two*.[34]

And to this theory of umpirage is due the strongest and most authoritative expression which the idea that the reserved powers of the States are unaffected by the principle of national supremacy and hence comprise an independent limit to otherwise constitutional acts of the National Government, has ever received. In fact, it is *so* strong that there is good reason for believing, as we shall see, that it was not intended to mean what it says. The reference is to Justice Nelson's opinion for the

[34] See especially Taney's opinions in *Ableman v. Booth*, 21 How. 506 (1859); and in *Gordon v. United States* (1864), published posthumously in 117 U.S. 697.

Court in *Collector v. Day*,[35] in which the Court held that a national income tax, in itself valid, could not be constitutionally levied upon State official salaries. The relevant portion of the opinion reads:

It is a familiar rule of construction of the Constitution of the Union, that the sovereign powers vested in the State governments by their respective Constitutions, remained unaltered and unimpaired, except so far as they were granted to the government of the United States. That the intention of the framers of the Constitution in this respect might not be misunderstood, this rule of interpretation is expressly declared in the tenth article of the amendments, namely: "The powers not delegated to the United States are reserved to the States respectively, or, to the people." The government of the United States, therefore, can claim no powers which are not granted to it by the Constitution, and the powers actually granted must be such as are expressly given, or given by necessary implication.

The general government, and the States, although both exist within the same territorial limits, are separate and distinct sovereignties, acting separately and independently of each other, within their respective spheres. The former in its appropriate sphere is supreme; but the States within the limits of their powers not granted, or, in the language of the Tenth Amendment, "reserved," are as independent of the general government as that government within its sphere is independent of the States.

The relations existing between the two governments are well stated by the present Chief Justice in the case of *Lane County v. Oregon*. "Both the States and the United States," he observed, "existed before the Constitution. The people, through that instrument, estab-

[35] 11 Wall. 113 (1871).

lished a more perfect union, by substituting a national government, acting with ample powers directly upon the citizens, instead of the confederate government, which acted with powers greatly restricted, only upon the States. But, in many of the articles of the Constitution, the necessary existence of the States, and within their proper spheres, the independent authority of the States, are distinctly recognized. To them nearly the whole charge of interior regulation is committed or left; to them, and to the people, all powers, not expressly delegated to the national government, are reserved." Upon looking into the Constitution it will be found that but a few of the articles in that instrument could be carried into practical effect without the existence of the States.

Two of the great departments of the government, the executive and legislative, depend upon the exercise of the powers, or upon the people of the States. The Constitution guarantees to the States a republican form of government, and protects each against invasion or domestic violence. Such being the separate and independent condition of the States in our complex system, as recognized by the Constitution, and the existence of which is so indispensable, that, without them, the general government itself would disappear from the family of nations, it would seem to follow, as a reasonable, if not a necessary consequence, that the means and instrumentalities employed for carrying on the operations of their governments, for preserving their existence, and fulfilling the high and responsible duties assigned to them in the Constitution, should be left free and unimpaired, should not be liable to be crippled, much less defeated by the taxing power of another government, which power acknowledges no limits but the will of the legislative body imposing the tax. And, more especially, those means and instrumentalities which are the creation of their sovereign and reserved rights, one of which is the establishment of the judicial department, and the appointment of officers to administer their laws. Without this power, and the exercise of it, we risk nothing in saying that no one of the States under the form of government guaranteed by the Constitution could long preserve its existence. A despotic government might. We have said that one of the reserved powers was that to establish a judicial department; it would have been more accurate, and in accordance with the existing state of things at the time, to have said the power to maintain a judicial department. All of the thirteen States were in the possession of this power, and had exercised it at the adoption of the Constitution; and it is not pretended that any grant of it to the general government is found in that instrument. It is, therefore, one of the sovereign powers vested in the States by their Constitutions, which remain unaltered and unimpaired, and in respect to which the State is as independent of the general government as that government is independent of the States.

The supremacy of the general government, therefore, so much relied on in the argument of the counsel for the plaintiff in error, in respect to the question before us, cannot be maintained. The two governments are upon an equality, and the question is whether the power "to lay and collect taxes" enables the general government to tax the salary of a judicial officer of the State, which officer is a means or instrumentality employed to carry into execution one of its most important functions, the administration of the laws, and which concerns the exercise of a right reserved to the States?[36]

Two questions arise on this language: first, does it *support* Proposition IV; secondly, does it—considering its context—*require* Proposi-

[36] ibid., 124-7.

tion IV? The answer to the first question is
clearly, yes; the answer to the second question
is, it is submitted, no. The essential question
with which the Court was dealing in *Collector
v. Day* was the *right of the people of a State to
maintain an autonomous, independently func-
tioning government along American lines, and
not at all the scope of the powers of such a government in relation to the supreme powers of the
National Government.* The full intention of the
holding could have been realized by basing it
on the guaranty of Article IV, section 4, of "a
republican form of government" to the States.
This is, in fact, mentioned by Justice Nelson,
but was unfortunately not made the basis of
the decision, probably because of the holding
in *Luther v. Borden*,[37] that what is "a republican
form of government" is *a political question.*
But a question which is "political" in one case,
may be justiciable in another. Regarded as an
interpretation of the Tenth Amendment, Justice Nelson's sweeping language is obviously
absurd, being neither more nor less than an
attempt to repeal the supremacy clause by
judicial fiat.[38]

Five years after *Collector v. Day*, Proposition
IV underwent a decided set-back, if not complete reversal, in the very field of power in

[37] 7 How. 1 (1848).
[38] See, in confirmance of above, Chief Justice Chase's opinions
for the Court in *Texas v. White*, 7 Wall. 700 (1869); and in *Veazie
Bank v. Fenno*, 8 Wall. 533, 547 (1869).

which it was originally promulgated in *New York v. Miln.* The reference is to *Henderson v. New York,*[39] in which the Miln decision was practically overturned. The following paragraphs from J. Miller's opinion for the unanimous Court tell the story:

Assuming, that, in the formation of our government, certain powers necessary to the administration of their internal affairs are reserved to the States, and that among these powers are those for the preservation of good order, of the health and comfort of the citizens, and their protection against pauperism and against contagious and infectious diseases, and other matters of legislation of like character, they insist that the power here exercised falls within this class, and belongs rightfully to the States.

This power, frequently referred to in the decisions of this Court, has been, in general terms, somewhat loosely called the police power. It is not necessary for the course of this discussion to attempt to define it more accurately than it has been defined already. It is not necessary, because whatever may be the nature and extent of that power, where not otherwise restricted, no definition of it, and no urgency for its use, can authorize a State to exercise it in regard to a subject-matter which has been confined exclusively to the discretion of Congress by the Constitution.

Nothing is gained in the argument by calling it the police power. Very many statutes, when the authority on which their enactments rest is examined, may be referred to different sources of power, and supported equally well under any of them. A statute may at the same time be an exercise of the taxing power and of the power of eminent domain. A statute punishing counterfeiting may be for the protection of the private citizen

[39] 92 U.S. 259 (1875).

against fraud, and a measure for the protection of the currency and for the safety of the government which issues it. It must occur very often that the shading which marks the line between one class of legislation and another is very nice, and not easily distinguishable.

But, however difficult this may be, it is clear, from the nature of our complex form of government, that, whenever the statute of a State invades the domain of legislation which belongs exclusively to the Congress of the United States, it is void, no matter under what class of powers it may fall, or how closely allied to powers conceded to belong to the States.

"It has been contended," says Marshall C. J., "that if a law passed by a State, in the exercise of its acknowledged sovereignty, comes into conflict with a law passed by Congress in pursuance of the Constitution, they affect the subject and each other like equal opposing powers. But the framers of our Constitution foresaw this state of things, and provided for it by declaring the supremacy, not only of itself, but of the laws made in pursuance thereof. The nullity of any act inconsistent with the Constitution is produced by the declaration that the Constitution is supreme." Where the Federal government has acted, he says, "In every such case the act of Congress or the treaty is supreme; and the laws of the State, though enacted in the exercise of powers not controverted, must yield to it." 9 Wheat. 210.[40]

While there is here some flavor of the Taney theory of mutually exclusive powers, yet it is clearly indicated that the national commercial power is to be defined entirely independently of the consideration that the States possess what is called the "police powers."

[40] *ibid.*, 271-2.

And in his opinion for the Court ten years later, in *New Orleans Gas Co. v. Louisiana Light Co.*,[41] Justice Harlan again sounds the Marshall note.

In the *Slaughter-House Cases*, 16 Wall. 36, 62, it was said that the police power is, from its nature, incapable of any exact definition or limitation; and, in *Stone v. Mississippi*, 101 U.S. 814, 818, that it is "easier to determine whether a particular case comes within the general scope of the power than to give an abstract definition of the power itself, which will be in all respects accurate." That there is a power, sometimes called the police power, which has never been surrendered by the States, in virtue of which they may, within certain limits, control everything within their respective territories, and upon the proper exercise of which, under some circumstances, may depend the public health, the public morals, or the public safety, is conceded in all the cases. *Gibbons v. Ogden*, 9 Wheat. 1,203. In its broadest sense, as sometimes defined, it includes all legislation and almost every function of civil government. *Barbier v. Connolly*, 113 U.S. 27, 31. As thus defined, we may, not improperly, refer to that power the authority of the State to create educational and charitable institutions, and provide for the establishment, maintenance, and control of public highways, turnpike roads, canals, wharves, ferries and telegraph lines, and the draining of swamps. Definitions of the police power must, however, be taken, subject to the condition that the State cannot, in its exercise, for any purpose whatever, encroach upon the powers of the general government, or rights granted or secured by the supreme law of the land.

Illustrations of interference with the rightful authority of the general government by State legislation

[41] 115 U.S. 650.

which was defended upon the ground that it was enacted under the police power, are found in cases where enactments concerning the introduction of foreign paupers, convicts, and diseased persons, were held to be unconstitutional, as conflicting, by their necessary operation and effect, with the paramount authority of Congress to regulate commerce with foreign nations, and among the several States. In *Henderson, &c. v. Mayor of New York*, 92 U.S. 259, the Court, speaking by Mr. Justice Miller, while declining to decide whether in the absence of action by Congress, the States can, or how far they may, by appropriate legislation protect themselves against paupers, vagrants, criminals and diseased persons, arriving from foreign countries, said, that no definition of the police power, and "no urgency for its use can authorize a State to exercise it in regard to a subject matter which has been confided exclusively to the discretion of Congress by the Constitution." *Chy Lung v. Freeman*, 92 U.S. 275.[42]

And to the same effect is the review of cases given by Justice Brewer, in his opinion for the Court in *Keller v. United States*,[43] a quarter of a century later. He says:

In *Gulf, C. & S. F. R. Co. v. Hefley*, 158 U.S. 98, 104, 39 L. ed. 910, 912, the rule is stated in these words:

Generally it may be said, in respect to laws of this character, that, though resting upon the police power of the State, they must yield whenever Congress, in the exercise of the powers granted to it, legislates upon the precise subject-matter, for that power, like all other reserved powers of the States, is subordinate to those in terms conferred by the Constitution upon the nation. "No urgency for its use can authorize a State to exer-

[42] *ibid.*, 661-2.
[43] 213 U.S. 139 (1909).

cise it in regard to a subject-matter which has been confided exclusively to the discretion of Congress by the Constitution." *Henderson v. New York* (*Henderson v. Wickham*), 92 U.S. 259, 271. "Definitions of the police power must, however, be taken subject to the condition that the State cannot, in its exercise, for any purpose whatever, encroach upon the powers of the general government, or rights granted or secured by the supreme law of the land." *New Orleans Gaslight Co. v. Louisiana Light & H. P. & Mfg. Co.*, 115 U.S. 650, 661. "While it may be a police power in the sense that all provisions for the health, comfort, and security of the citizens are police regulations, and an exercise of the police power, it has been said more than once in this Court that, where such powers are so exercised as to come within the domain of Federal authority as defined by the Constitution, the latter must prevail." *Morgan's L. & T. R. & S. S. Co. v. Board of Health*, 118 U.S. 455, 464.

See also *Lottery Case* (*Champion v. Ames*), 188 U.S. 321.

That there is a moral consideration in the special facts of this case, that the act charged is within the scope of the police power, is immaterial, for, as stated, there is in the Constitution no grant to Congress of the police power. And the legislation must stand or fall according to the determination of the question of the power of Congress to control generally dealings of citizens with aliens. In other words, an immense body of legislation, which heretofore has been recognized as peculiarly within the jurisdiction of the States, may be taken by Congress away from them. Although Congress has not largely entered into this field of legislation, it may do so, if it has the power. Then we should be brought face to face with such a change in the internal conditions of this country as was never dreamed of by the framers of the Constitution. While the acts of Congress are to be liberally construed in order to enable it to carry into effect the powers conferred, it is equally true that prohibitions and limitations upon those powers should also be fairly and reasonably enforced. *Fairbank v. United States*, 181 U.S. 283. To exaggerate in the one direction and restrict in the other will tend to substitute one consolidated government for the present Federal system. We should never forget the declaration in *Texas v. White*, 7 Wall. 700, 725, that "the Constitution, in all its provisions, looks to an indestructible Union, composed of indestructible states."[44]

But here, in Justice Brewer's *own words*, we perceive a veering of the judicial mind back toward Proposition IV. What he says, in effect, is that, just because Congress's powers are supreme when they conflict with the reserved powers of the States, the Court should be very slow to construe Congress's powers so broadly as to project them into what in the past has been the customary field of action of the States, otherwise the "federal equilibrium" will be upset. This suggestion has subsequently borne important fruit at times, in the shape of special interpretative *devices* meant to secure the practical results of Proposition IV without incurring the logical objections to this Proposition. One of these will be pointed out shortly.

4. *PRESENT CONFUSION*

Beginning about 1890 the United States Supreme Court, along with the rest of the country, became indoctrinated with the the-

[44] *ibid.*, 146-9.

ories of *laissez faire*, which boil down to the idea that the less government interferes with business the better for all. Already, before this date, the Court had firmly established the doctrine that Congress's power under the commerce clause is as to most important matters an *exclusive* power. The consequence of this doctrine is that any State law which, in the judgment of the Court, affects interstate commerce to such an extent as to "regulate" it, is *ipso facto* void. This doctrine has been highly beneficial in permitting business interests to spread over the country without much regard to State lines.

On the other hand, when Congress, with the enactment of the Sherman Act in 1890, began to evince a disposition to actively exercise its power under the commerce clause for the purpose of regulating business, the Court proceeded to set up State power as a limit upon Congressional power. Thus, the *laissez faire* principle was given a formulation in constitutional law which enabled the Court to work it both ways. When a State in professed exercise of its reserved powers passed a law regulative of business and the Court found it to impinge directly on interstate business, the law was pronounced void on the ground of interfering with Congress's power over commerce among the States. Conversely, when Congress in professed exercise of its power to regulate commerce among the States, passed legislation

which impinged directly upon certain processes of business which the Court held to be
local, the act was pronounced void as an interference with the reserved powers of the States.
*And the total result of this kind of reasoning was
the appearance of a no-man's land in which business interests organized on a national scale at
times escape all regulation.*[45]

The initial case illustrative of the Court's
new ideology so far as it affected Congressional
legislation was the famous Sugar Trust[46] decision early in 1895. Here the Anti-Trust Act
was held not to apply to a combination of
sugar refiners who were conceded to control
98% of that necessary of life in the United
States. The Court's point of departure is indicated by the following extracts from Chief
Justice Fuller's opinion:

The fundamental question is, whether conceding
that the existence of a monopoly in manufacture is
established by the evidence, that monopoly can be
directly suppressed under the act of Congress in the
mode attempted by this bill.

It cannot be denied that the power of a State to
protect the lives, health, and property of its citizens,
and to preserve good order and the public morals,
"the power to govern men and things within the limits
of its dominion," is a power originally and always belonging to the States, not surrendered by them to the
general government, nor directly restrained by the
Constitution of the United States, and essentially ex-

[45] See the present writer's *Twilight of the Supreme Court* (1934),
pp. 18-20, 34-5, 49.
[46] *United States v. E. C. Knight Co.*, 156 U.S. 1.

clusive. The relief of the citizens of each State from the burden of monopoly and the evils resulting from the restraint of trade among such citizens was left with the States to deal with, and this Court has recognized their possession of that power even to the extent of holding that an employment or business carried on by private individuals, when it becomes a matter of such public interest and importance as to create a common charge or burden upon the citizen; in other words, when it becomes a practical monopoly, to which the citizen is compelled to resort and by means of which a tribute can be exacted from the community, is subject to regulation by State legislative power. On the other hand, the power of Congress to regulate commerce among the several States is also exclusive. The Constitution does not provide that interstate commerce shall be free, but, by the grant of this exclusive power to regulate it, it was left free except as Congress might impose restraints. Therefore it has been determined that the failure of Congress to exercise this exclusive power in any case is an expression of its will that the subject shall be free from restrictions or impositions upon it by the several States, and if a law passed by a State in the exercise of its acknowledged powers comes into conflict with that will, the Congress and the State cannot occupy the position of equal opposing sovereignties, because the Constitution declares its supremacy and that of the laws passed in pursuance thereof; and that which is not supreme must yield to that which is supreme. . . .

It is vital that the independence of the commercial power and of the police power, and the delimitation between them, however sometimes perplexing, should always be recognized and observed, for while the one furnishes the strongest bond of union, the other is essential to the preservation of the autonomy of the States as required by our dual form of government; and acknowledged evils, how ever grave and urgent they may appear to be, had better be borne, than the risk be run, in the effort to suppress them, of more serious consequences by resort to expedients of even doubtful constitutionality.[47]

Thus again we encounter the thought that just because Congress's power to regulate commerce among the States *is* supreme over State power, it must be so construed as not to conflict with State power. And pursuing this line of thought, the Court reached the following result:

Contracts [said Chief Justice Fuller], combinations, or conspiracies to control domestic enterprise in manufacture, agriculture, mining, production in all its forms, or to raise or lower prices or wages, might unquestionably tend to restrain external as well as domestic trade, but the restraint would be an indirect result, however inevitable, and whatever its extent, and such result would not necessarily determine the object of the contract, combination, or conspiracy. . . . Slight reflection will show that, if the national power extends to all contracts and combinations in manufacture, agriculture, mining, and other productive industries, whose ultimate result may affect external commerce, comparatively little of business operations and affairs would be left for State control.[48]

To put the same idea more briefly, the effects of a combination of producers upon commerce among the States in the product must be labelled "indirect" *however inevitable they may be and however extensive*, and with that label affixed such effects are put beyond

[47] *ibid.*, 11-13.
[48] *ibid.*, 16.

Congress's power over commerce among the States, because otherwise there would be little in the way of business for the States to regulate. But why would this result follow? The opinion does not say, but the answer would seem to lie in the Court's tacit recognition that *the tie-up between commerce among the States and production is today both inevitable and extensive.* In short, the term "indirect" in this context is a mere *device*, a *formula* pulled out of the judicial hat, for the purpose of "shooing" away what the Court itself appears to recognize as an altogether natural and logical extension of the national commercial power. We shall return to the subject in the following chapter.

We now turn to two lines of cases in which the Court arrived practically synchronously at precisely opposite results with respect to Proposition IV. The first line has to do with railway rate regulation. That the power to regulate the local rates of carriers is one of the reserved powers of the State was established by scores of cases in 1913, and indeed is still the law today. Yet this fact, Justice Hughes pointed out in his opinion for the Court in the Minnesota Rate Cases,[49] did not mean that Congress might not exert its supreme power in the same field. Thus, quoting Marshall's statement in *Gibbons v. Ogden*, that "the com-

[49] 230 U.S. 353 (1913).

pletely internal commerce of a State, then, may be considered as reserved for the State itself," Justice Hughes said:

This reservation to the States manifestly is only of that authority which is consistent with and not opposed to the grant to Congress. There is no room in our scheme of government for the assertion of state power in hostility to the authorized exercise of Federal power. The authority of Congress extends to every part of interstate commerce, and to every instrumentality or agency by which it is carried on; and the full control by Congress of the subjects committed to its regulation is not to be denied or thwarted by the commingling of interstate and intrastate operations. This is not to say that the Nation may deal with the internal concerns of the State, as such, but that the execution by Congress of its constitutional power to regulate interstate commerce is not limited by the fact that intrastate transactions may have become so interwoven therewith that the effective government of the former incidentally controls the latter. This conclusion necessarily results from the supremacy of the national power within its appointed sphere. *McCulloch v. Maryland*, 4 Wheat. 316, 405, 426; *The Daniel Ball*, 10 Wall. 557, 565; *Smith v. Alabama*, 124 U.S. 465, 473; *Baltimore & Ohio R. R. Co. v. Interstate Commerce Commission*, 221 U.S. 612, 618, 619; *Southern Railway Co. v. United States*, 222 U.S. 20, 26, 27; *Mondou v. N. Y., N. H., & H. R. R. Co.*, 223 U.S. 1, 47, 54, 55.[50]

And in the Shreveport Case,[51] the year following, the Court sustained a certain regulation of local rates by the Interstate Commerce Commission on the ground that it was essential

[50] *ibid.*, 398-9.
[51] 234 U.S. 342.

to protect the interstate rates of the carriers affected. Said Justice Hughes, again speaking for the Court:

Its [Congress] authority extending to these interstate carriers as instrumentalities of interstate commerce, necessarily embraces the right to control their operations in all matters having such a close and substantial relation to interstate traffic that the control is essential or appropriate to the security of that traffic, to the efficiency of the interstate service, and to the maintenance of conditions under which interstate commerce may be conducted upon fair terms and without molestation or hindrance. . . . Wherever the interstate and intrastate transactions of carriers are so related that the government of the one involves the control of the other, it is Congress, and not the State, that is entitled to prescribe the final and dominant rule, for otherwise Congress would be denied the exercise of its constitutional authority and the State, and not the nation, would be supreme within the national field.[52]

Referring to this decision a few months later, Justice Hughes said, in a public address:

Within its sphere as recognized by the Constitution, the Nation is supreme. The question is simply of the Federal power as granted, where there is authorized exercise of that power, there is no reserved power to nullify it—a principle obviously essential to our national integrity, yet continually calling for new applications.[53]

By the Transportation Act of 1920 Congress extended considerably the principle of the

[52] *ibid.*, 351-2.
[53] Address before New York State Bar Association, January 14, 1916; 39 *Reps. N.Y. Bar Ass'n*, 266, 275.

Shreveport decision for the protection of the railroads, and was sustained by the Court in so doing.[54]

The other line of cases just referred to brings us into contact once more with Justice, later Chief Justice, White's crusade, mentioned in Chapter II, for the rescue of the Federal System from an engulfing nationalism. Following his dictum in *Buttfield v. Stranahan*, White got his next chance to strike a blow for the sacred cause as a dissenter in the Northern Securities Case.[55] In his argument of the case for the government Attorney General Knox had said:

Congress having the police power, or its equivalent, over foreign and interstate commerce and the instrumentalities thereof, may in exercising it, strike down restraints upon such commerce, whether they result from combinations and monopolies of the agencies of transportation or otherwise, just as a State could prohibit similar restraints upon intrastate commerce. To contend otherwise is to contend that the Federal power over interstate and foreign commerce is not supreme, but is in some respects subordinate to State authority; that the police powers or the reserved powers of the States are, for some purposes, paramount to the powers of Congress in fields wherein the Federal Government has been invested by the Constitution with complete and supreme authority. This, of course, is not so. *New Orleans Gas Co. v. Louisiana Light Co.*, 115 U.S. 650, 661.[56]

---

[54] *Wisconsin v. C. B. & Q. R. R.*, 257 U.S. 563 (1922).
[55] 193 U.S. 197 (1904).
[56] *ibid.*, 307.

Justice White's retort to this type of reasoning is to be seen in the following extracts from his dissenting opinion:

The contention broadly is that Congress has not only the authority to regulate the exercise of interstate commerce, but under that power has the right to regulate the ownership and possession of property, if the enjoyment of such rights would enable those who possessed them if they engaged in interstate commerce to exert a power over the same. . . . Under this doctrine the sum of property to be acquired by individuals or by corporations, the contracts which they may make, would be within the regulating power of Congress. If it were judged by Congress that the farmer in sowing his crops should be limited to a certain production because overproduction would give power to affect commerce, Congress could regulate that subject. If the acquisition of a large amount of property by an individual was deemed by Congress to confer upon him the power to affect interstate commerce if he engaged in it, Congress could regulate that subject. If the wage-earner organized to better his condition and Congress believed that the existence of such organization would give power, if it were exerted, to affect interstate commerce, Congress could forbid the organization of all labor associations. Indeed, the doctrine must in reason lead to a concession of the right in Congress to regulate concerning the aptitude, the character and capacity of persons. If individuals were deemed by Congress to be possessed of such ability that participation in the management of two great competing railroad enterprises would endow them with the power to injuriously affect interstate commerce, Congress could forbid such participation. If the principle were adopted, and the power which would arise from so doing were exercised, the result would be not only to destroy the State and Federal governments, but by the implication of authority, from which the destruction would be brought about, there would be erected upon the ruins of both a government endowed with the arbitrary power to disregard the great guaranty of life, liberty and property and every other safeguard upon which organized civil society depends. I say the guaranty, because in my opinion the three are indissolubly united, and one cannot be destroyed without the other. Of course, to push propositions to the extreme to which they naturally lead is often an unsafe guide. But at the same time the conviction cannot be escaped by me that principles and conduct bear a relation one to the other, especially in matters of public concern. The fathers founded our government upon an enduring basis of right, principle and of limitation of power. Destroy the principles and the limitations which they imposed, and I am unable to say that conduct may not, when unrestrained, give rise to action doing violence to the great truths which the destroyed principles embodied.[57]

Four years later Justice White was able to persuade a majority of the Court to pronounce void the first Employers' Liability Act in deference to his point of view. The pertinent portion of his opinion follows:

It remains only to consider the contention which we have previously quoted, that the act is constitutional, although it embraces subjects not within the power of Congress to regulate commerce, because one who engages in interstate commerce thereby submits all his business concerns to the regulating power of Congress. To state the proposition is to refute it. It assumes that because one engages in interstate commerce he thereby endows Congress with power not delegated to it by the Constitution, in other words, with the right to legislate concerning matters of purely State concern. It rests

[57] *ibid.*, 396-8.

upon the conception that the Constitution destroyed that freedom of commerce which it was its purpose to preserve, since it treats the right to engage in interstate commerce as a privilege which cannot be availed of except upon such conditions as Congress may prescribe, even although the conditions would be otherwise beyond the power of Congress. It is apparent that if the contention were well founded it would extend the power of Congress to every conceivable subject, however inherently local, would obliterate all the limitations of power imposed by the Constitution, and would destroy the authority of the States as to all conceivable matters which from the beginning have been, and must continue to be, under their control so long as the Constitution endures.[58]

And in the Commodities Clause Case of 1909,[59] White again triumphed to the extent of inducing the Court to curtail the literal meaning of the act of Congress involved. "Conceding" the plenitude of Congress's power over commerce, and the principle that it "must remain free from restrictions and limitations arising or asserted to arise by State laws, whether enacted before or after Congress has chosen to exert its lawful power to regulate," he went on nevertheless to say:

If the contentions of the government as to the meaning of the commodities clause be well founded, at least a majority of the Court are of the opinion that we may not avoid determining the following grave constitutional questions: 1. Whether the power of Congress to regulate commerce embraces the authority to control or prohibit the mining, manufacturing, production or

---

[58] *Employers' Liability Cases*, 207 U.S. 463, 502-3 (1908).
[59] *United States v. Delaware and Hudson Co.*, 213 U.S. 366 (1909).

ownership of any article or commodity, not because of some inherent quality of the commodity, but simply because it may become the subject of interstate commerce. 2. If the right to regulate commerce does not thus extend, can it be impliedly made to embrace subjects which it does not control, by forbidding a railroad company engaged in interstate commerce from carrying lawful articles or commodities because, at some time prior to the transportation, it had manufactured, mined, produced or owned them, etc.? And involved in the determination of the foregoing questions we shall necessarily be called upon to decide, (a) Did the adoption of the Constitution and the grant of power to Congress to regulate commerce have the effect of depriving the States of the authority to endow a carrier with the attribute of producing as well as transporting particular commodities, a power which the States from the beginning have freely exercised, and by the exertion of which governmental power the resources of the several States have been developed, their enterprises fostered, and vast investments of capital have been made possible? (b) Although the government of the United States, both within its spheres of national and local legislative power, has in the past for public purposes, either expressly or impliedly, authorized the manufacture, mining, production and carriage of commodities by one and the same railway corporation, was the exertion of such power beyond the scope of the authority of Congress, or, what is equivalent thereto [*sic*], was its exercise but a mere license, subject at any time to be revoked and completely destroyed by means of a regulation of Congress?

While the grave questions thus stated must necessarily, as we have said, arise for decision, if the contention of the government, as to the meaning of the commodities clause be correct, we do not intend, by stating them, to decide them, or even in the slightest degree to presently intimate, in any respect whatever, an opinion upon them. It will be time enough to approach their consideration if we are compelled to do so hereafter, as the result of the further analysis, which we propose to make in order to ascertain the meaning of the commodities clause.

It is elementary when the constitutionality of a statute is assailed, if the statute be reasonably susceptible of two interpretations, by one of which it would be unconstitutional and by the other valid, it is our plain duty to adopt that construction which will save the statute from constitutional infirmity.[60]

And it was upon these dicta that counsel opposing the National Child Labor Act, under review in *Hammer v. Dagenhart*, mainly relied. The following is a pertinent extract from brief for appellees:

There is practically involved in this case the right of Congress to regulate, under the guise of a commerce regulation, every relation of life. . . . If the views of those who assert the constitutionality of this method are sound, there is no practical necessity, nor reason, for State legislatures, and certainly none for constitutional amendments. Of course we may have a minimum wage law, applicable to all industries, passed on the demand of organized or unorganized labor, by the simple Congressional enactment that no factory may tender goods for interstate shipment which does not pay a minimum scale of wages. If Congress conceived that the use of commercial fertilizers is not so good for the permanent prosperity of the country as the slower processes of vegetable fertilization, then it may prevent the wheat produced by commercial fertilizers from being shipped in interstate trade. More than that, and we protest that it is not fanciful, but under the terms of this statute directly involved, Congress may

[60] *ibid.*, 406-7.

by the same token, and without amendment to the Constitution, enact complete prohibition of the liquor traffic by forbidding personal travel or shipment of goods by any man who, within thirty days previous to such travel, or shipment, has taken a drink of whiskey.

We do not believe with those who hold that there has been a discovery of a new instrument, whereby Congress may take over the entire control of processes of production, matters of personal morals and decency, and the other regulative powers that have, since the foundation of our government, been asserted and assumed to be included in the police power in, and reserved to, the States.[61]

There are two principal answers to this type of argument. In the first place, there is, obviously, no "real and substantial relation" between a man's drinking to excess, or at all, and his engaging in interstate commerce, whereas *interstate traffic* in child labor goods is the inducing cause of the child labor evil. The right of persons to use the facilities of interstate commerce for reasons that have nothing to do with commerce in the basic sense of *traffic* and *dealing* is one thing; the right of *producers* to use such facilities to secure access to the *interstate market* is quite a different thing. The Constitution does not limit the power to regulate commerce among the States by the requirement that the interstate market be kept open to those who employ degraded and destructive methods either in the production or the disposal of goods, any

[61] *loc. cit.*, 16.

more than it limits the police power of the States by a similar requirement as to the local market. Nor is there any more reason why a business corporation chartered, say by Delaware, should be regarded as having access to the *interstate* market without the consent of Congress than that it should be entitled to enter a sister State without its consent to engage in local business there.

Furthermore, should Congress ever make up its mind to keep drunkards off the trains—or people heading for Reno or Little Rock[62]—a reversal of *Hammer v. Dagenhart* would not lend half the support to its efforts as is already obtainable from the decision in *Hoke v. United States*, sustaining the Mann White Slave Act, which in fact affords the basis of the present-day extraordinary intervention of the National Government in the field of criminal law enforcement.[63]

[62] Appellees' Brief (p. 26) had also conjured up the possibility of Congress using the power claimed for it in *Hammer v. Dagenhart* to regulate divorce.

[63] In his dissent, for himself and three associates in the Lottery Case, 188 U.S. 321 Chief Justice Fuller had remarked: "Nobody would pretend that persons could be kept off the trains because they were going from one State to another to engage in the lottery business." *ibid.*, 374. The results reached in such cases as *Hoke v. United States* and *Brooks v. United States*, 267 U.S. 432 (1925), in which the Stolen Automobile Act of 1919 was sustained, compel a smile at the former Chief Justice's confident tone. A current proposal would make it a crime against the United States to send "doped" race horses from one State to another. *New York Times*, March 29, 1936. Meantime, the gangsters are preparing, in reliance on the Poultry Case, to challenge the constitutionality of the "Lindbergh Law." *ibid.*, July 5 and November 3, 1935.

But the second answer to the type of reasoning indulged in by both Court and counsel in the above quoted passages is perhaps the more important one. It is the answer which is made by Justice Stone for himself and Justices Brandeis and Cardozo in the recent case of *United States v. Butler*, and is given at length at the end of Chapter VII.[64]

It seems, therefore, that Proposition IV is only one of a pair of horses which the Court has ready saddled and bridled, depending on the direction it wishes to ride—the other being the supremacy clause of the Constitution itself. Nor have more recent judicial utterances contributed to clarify this confusion of doctrine. Some further dicta bearing on the matter follow:

(1) Congress may exercise this authority [over interstate commerce] in aid of the policy of the State, if it sees fit to do so. It is equally clear that the policy of Congress acting independently of the States may induce legislation without reference to the particular policy or law of any given State. . . . The control of Congress over interstate commerce is not to be limited by State laws.[65]

These words were spoken for the Court a little over seven months after the decision in *Hammer v. Dagenhart* and by the same Justice.

[64] *ibid., infra*, pp. 247-9.
[65] *United States v. Hill*, 248 U.S. 420, 425 (1919).

(2) And the same Justice was again spokesman for the Court in *United States v. Doremus*,[66] in which the Harrison Narcotic Act was sustained against the objection that it invaded State powers. He said:

Of course Congress may not in the exercise of federal power exert authority wholly reserved to the States. Many decisions of this Court have so declared. And from an early day the Court has held that the fact that other motives may impel the exercise of federal taxing power does not authorize the Courts to inquire into that subject. If the legislation enacted has some reasonable relation to the exercise of the taxing authority conferred by the Constitution, it cannot be invalidated because of the supposed motives which induced it. . . .

Nor is it sufficient to invalidate the taxing authority given to the Congress by the Constitution that the same business may be regulated by the police power of the State.[67]

(3) Later, however, in *Linder v. United States*,[68] the operation of this act was curtailed by a decision which was based in part upon the following language by Justice McReynolds:

Congress cannot, under the pretext of executing delegated power, pass laws for the accomplishment of objects not intrusted to the Federal Government. And we accept as established doctrine that any provision of an act of Congress ostensibly enacted under power granted by the Constitution, not naturally and reasonably adapted to the effective exercise of such power, but solely to the achievement of something plainly

---

[66] *United States v. Doremus*, 249 U.S. 86 (1919).
[67] *ibid.*, 93-4.
[68] 268 U.S. 5 (1925).

within power reserved to the States, is invalid and cannot be enforced. *McCulloch v. Maryland*, 4 Wheat. 316, 423, *License Tax Cases*, 5 Wall. 462, *United States v. Dewitt*, 9 Wall. 41, *Keller v. United States*, 213 U.S. 138, *Hammer v. Dagenhart*, 247 U.S. 251, *Child Labor Tax Case*, 259 U.S. 20.[69]

At the same time Justice McReynolds took occasion to insinuate that, in view of more recent decisions than the Doremus Case the whole Narcotic Act was probably unconstitutional; but when in the Nigro Case[70] the narcotic interests acted on this hint, the Court—Justices McReynolds, Sutherland, and Butler dissenting—refused to deliver the goods.

(4) Meantime, in *Everard's Breweries v. Day*,[71] in which the National Prohibition Act was involved, the Court, speaking by Justice Sanford, answered the argument that "the grant of power [to Congress] contained in the Eighteenth Amendment is limited by the reservations of the Tenth Amendment as follows":

It is clear that if the act is within the authority delegated to Congress by the Eighteenth Amendment, its validity is not impaired by reason of any power reserved to the States. The words "concurrent power" as used in the second section of the Amendment "do not mean joint power, or require that legislation thereunder by Congress, to be effective, shall be approved or sanctioned by the several States or any of them"; and the power confided to Congress, while not ex-

[69] *ibid.*, 17.
[70] 276 U.S. 332 (1928).
[71] 265 U.S. 545 (1924).

clusive, "is in no wise dependent on or affected by action or inaction on the part of the several States or any of them." *National Prohibition Cases*, 253 U.S. 350, 387. And if the act is within the power confided to Congress, the Tenth Amendment by its very terms, has no application, since it only reserves to the States "powers not delegated to the United States by the Constitution." See *McCulloch v. Maryland*, 4 Wheat. 316, 406; *Lottery Case*, 188 U.S. 321, 357.[72]

Finally, reference should be made to the current case of *Whitefield v. Ohio*,[73] where the Court sustained the power of Congress to subject prison-made goods brought into a State from another State to the laws of the former following their arrival in the hands of the consignee. The holding is based on a revival of the Rahrer Case,[74] decided forty-five years ago, and the opinion of Justice Sutherland for the unanimous Court does not once mention *Hammer v. Dagenhart*, although the argument against the act under review was based altogether on that case.

To sum this and the preceding chapter up: From 1837 on judicial dicta began appearing which treated some of the reserved powers of the States as exclusive in nature and hence as capable of setting an independent limitation to the delegated powers of the United States. Prior to the Civil War the identity of such exclusive powers was most frequently indi-

[72] *ibid.*, 558.
[73] 80 Law. Ed. Advance Opinions, 527 (March 2, 1936).
[74] 140 U.S. 545.

cated by reference to certain *subject-matters*, especially those matters local control of which was of most immediate concern to the slavery interest. Thus the theory arose that such *subject-matters* had been put by the Tenth Amendment beyond the reach of the National Government, even though a definition of the delegated powers which was uninfluenced by this theory might extend to the subject-matters in question. After the Civil War this *modus loquendi* disappeared until quite recently, but its place was taken by a new practice which had meantime arisen, namely, that of describing the reserved powers of the States by reference to the *purposes* served by them, which were identified with the larger purposes of good government the world over; and on this basis was erected—in defiance of the Preamble of the Constitution—the theory that the delegated powers of the United States were designed to serve only a few comparatively narrow purposes, the chief one being *the advancement of commerce*.

The answer, however, is the same in both cases. The Tenth Amendment speaks only of *powers* and does not mention *fields* of power, *subjects* of power, *purposes* of power, and the like.[75] What is more, the supremacy clause

---

[75] As Professor Collier has excellently put it: "It is a fallacy to suppose that this amendment marks out particular subjects, like agricultural production, and designates them as exclusively within the State domain. It may well happen that the same subject can be reached both by powers exercised by the Federal Government

does not qualify the supremacy over conflicting State laws with which it endows laws of
the United States made in pursuance of the
Constitution, either by excepting State laws
which are made for certain *purposes* or those
which are enacted to govern certain *subjects*.
And if a State possesses a power it may exercise it by enacting a law, which then become
subject to the principle of national supremacy.
Clearly there are no dormant State powers
which are more potent to delimit national
power than are State powers which are exercised.

In short, *the terms of the Tenth Amendment
are logically insufficient to segregate to the States
any subject-matter whatsoever upon which governmental powers may operate, or any purpose
whatsoever in the promotion of which governmental power may be employed; and the terms of
the supremacy clause logically forbid any such
notion.*

The full force of this criticism will appear
in connection with the following chapter.

and also by powers exercised by the State Government. The subject, conceived of as a sort of entity, cannot be said to belong either
to the nation or to the States, exclusively." Chas. S. Collier, "Judicial Bootstraps and the General Welfare Clause, the A. A. A.
Opinion," reprinted from the January 1936 issue of the *George
Washington L. R.*, p. 14.

PROPOSITION V

PROPOSITION V

That production is a subject which is segregated to the reserved powers of the States and so lies outside the range of Congress's power to regulate commerce among the States.

1. *THE ORIGINAL FORM OF THIS ISSUE: THE TARIFF*

THAT a close relation exists between production and commerce was the basic assumption of Alexander Hamilton's famous Report on Manufactures, communicated to the House of Representatives December 5, 1791. In the following paragraph from this document Hamilton is suggesting a national system of inspection of manufactures intended for the foreign market:

This is not among the least important of the means by which the prosperity of manufactures may be promoted. It is, indeed, in many cases, one of the most essential. Contributing to prevent frauds upon consumers at home, and exporters to foreign countries; to improve the quality, and preserve the character of the national manufactures; it cannot fail to aid the expeditious and advantageous sale of them, and to serve as a guard against successful competition from other quarters. The reputation of the flour and lumber of some States, and of the potash of others, has been established by an attention to this point. And the like good name might be procured for those articles, wheresoever produced, by a judicious and uniform system of inspection, throughout the ports of the United States. A like system might also be extended with advantage to other commodities.[1]

The question of the constitutional power of the National Government to affect production within the States through its power to regulate commerce was first raised in the field of foreign commercial regulation, in connection with the protective tariff. Story's adequate summary of this once bitter controversy contains many observations that have bearing on current issues respecting the power of Congress to protect and assist productive industry. The relevant paragraphs from the second volume of the *Commentaries on the Constitution* follow:

Sec. 1079. The reasoning by which the doctrine is maintained, that the power to regulate commerce cannot be constitutionally applied, as a means directly to encourage domestic manufactures, has been in part already adverted to in considering the extent of the power to lay taxes. It is proper, however, to present it entire in its present connection. It is to the following effect: The Constitution is one of limited and enumerated powers; and none of them can be rightfully exercised beyond the scope of the objects specified in those powers. It is not disputed that when the power is given, all the appropriate means to carry it into effect are included. Neither is it disputed that the laying of duties is, or may be an appropriate means of regulating commerce. But the question is a very different one, whether, under pretense of an exercise of the power to regulate commerce, Congress may in fact impose duties

[1] *Works* (J. C. Hamilton, Ed.), III, 254-5.

for objects wholly distinct from commerce. The question comes to this, whether a power exclusively for the regulation of commerce is a power for the regulation of manufactures? The statement of such a question would seem to involve its own answer. Can a power granted for one purpose be transferred to another? If it can, where is the limitation in the Constitution? Are not commerce and manufactures as distinct as commerce and agriculture? If they are, how can a power to regulate one arise from a power to regulate the other? It is true that commerce and manufactures are, or may be, intimately connected with each other. A regulation of one may injuriously or beneficially affect the other. But that is not the point in controversy. It is, whether Congress has a right to regulate that which is not committed to it, under a power which is committed to it, simply because there is or may be an intimate connection between the powers. If this were admitted, the enumeration of the powers of Congress would be wholly unnecessary and nugatory. Agriculture, colonies, capital, machinery, the wages of labor, the profits of stock, the rents of land, the punctual performance of contracts, and the diffusion of knowledge, would all be within the scope of the power; for all of them bear an intimate relation to commerce. The result would be, that the powers of Congress would embrace the widest extent of legislative functions, to the utter demolition of all constitutional boundaries between the State and national governments. When duties are laid, not for purposes of revenue, but of retaliation and restriction, to countervail foreign restrictions, they are strictly within the scope of the power, as a regulation of commerce. But when laid to encourage manufactures, they have nothing to do with it. The power to regulate manufactures is no more confided to Congress than the power to interfere with the systems of education, the poor laws, or the road laws of the States. It is notorious that, in the convention, an attempt was made to intro-

duce into the Constitution a power to encourage manufactures; but it was withheld. Instead of granting the
power to Congress, permission was given to the States
to impose duties, with the consent of that body, to
encourage their own manufactures; and thus, in the
true spirit of justice, imposing the burden on those who
were to be benefited. It is true that Congress may,
incidentally, when laying duties for revenue, consult
the other interests of the country. They may so ar-
range the details as indirectly to aid manufactures.
And this is the whole extent to which Congress has ever
gone until the tariffs which have given rise to the
present controversy. The former precedents of Congress are not, even if admitted to be authoritative,
applicable to the question now presented.

Sec. 1080. The reasoning of those who maintain the
doctrine that Congress has authority to apply the
power to regulate commerce to the purpose of protecting and encouraging domestic manufactures, is to the
following effect: The power to regulate commerce being
in its terms unlimited, includes all means appropriate
to the end, and all means which have been usually
exerted under the power. No one can doubt or deny
that a power to regulate trade involves a power to tax
it. It is a familiar mode, recognized in the practice of all
nations, and was known and admitted by the United
States while they were colonies, and has ever since been
acted upon without opposition or question. The American colonies wholly denied the authority of the British
Parliament to tax them, except as a regulation of commerce; but they admitted this exercise of power as
legitimate and unquestionable. The distinction was
with difficulty maintained in practice between laws
for the regulation of commerce by way of taxation
and laws which were made for mere monopoly or restriction, when they incidentally produced revenue.
And it is certain that the main and admitted object of
parliamentary regulations of trade with the colonies

was the encouragement of manufactures in Great Britain. Other nations have, in like manner, for like purposes, exercised the like power. So that there is no novelty in the use of the power, and no stretch in the range of the power.

Sec. 1081. Indeed the advocates of the opposite doctrine admit that the power may be applied so as incidentally to give protection to manufactures, when revenue is the principal design; and that it may also be applied to countervail the injurious regulations of foreign powers, when there is no design of revenue. These concessions admit, then, that the regulations of commerce are not wholly for purposes of revenue, or wholly confined to the purposes of commerce, considered *per se*. If this be true, then other objects may enter into commercial regulations; and, if so, what restraint is there as to the nature or extent of the objects to which they may reach, which does not resolve itself into a question of expediency and policy? It may be admitted that a power given for one purpose cannot be perverted to purposes wholly opposite, or beside its legitimate scope. But what perversion is there in applying a power to the very purposes to which it has been usually applied? Under such circumstances, does not the grant of the power, without restriction, concede that it may be legitimately applied to such purposes? If a different intent had existed, would not that intent be manifested by some corresponding limitation?

Sec. 1082. Now it is well known that, in commercial and manufacturing nations the power to regulate commerce has embraced practically the encouragement of manufactures. It is believed that not a single exception can be named. So, in an especial manner, the power has always been understood in Great Britain, from which we derive our parentage, our laws, our language, and our notions upon commercial subjects. Such was confessedly the notion of the different States in the Union under the confederation, and before the formation of the present Constitution. One known object of the policy of the manufacturing States then was, the protection and encouragement of their manufactures by regulations of commerce. And the exercise of this power was a source of constant difficulty and discontent; not because improper of itself, but because it bore injuriously upon the commercial arrangements of other States. The want of uniformity in the regulations of commerce was a source of perpetual strife and dissatisfaction, of inequalities and rivalries, and retaliations among the States. When the Constitution was framed, no one ever imagined that the power of protection of manufactures was to be taken away from the States, and yet not delegated to the Union. The very suggestion would of itself have been fatal to the adoption of the Constitution. The manufacturing States would never have acceded to it upon any such terms; and they never could, without the power, have safely acceded to it, for it would have sealed their ruin. The same reasoning would apply to the agricultural States; for the regulation of commerce, with a view to encourage domestic agriculture, is just as important, and just as vital to the interests of the nation, and just as much an application of the power, as the protection or encouragement of manufactures. It would have been strange, indeed, if the people of the United States had been solicitous solely to advance and encourage commerce, with a total disregard of the interests of agriculture and manufactures, which had, at the time of the adoption of the Constitution, an unequivocal preponderance throughout the Union. It is manifest, from contemporaneous documents, that one object of the Constitution was to encourage manufactures and agriculture by this very use of the power.

Sec. 1083. The terms, then, of the Constitution are sufficiently large to embrace the power; the practice of other nations, and especially of Great Britain and of the American States, has been to use it in this manner; and this exercise of it was one of the very grounds upon which the establishment of the Constitution was urged and vindicated. The argument, then, in its favor would seem to be absolutely irresistible under this aspect. But there are other very weighty considerations which enforce it.

Sec. 1084. In the first place, if Congress does not possess the power to encourage domestic manufactures by regulations of commerce, the power is annihilated for the whole nation. The States are deprived of it; they have made a voluntary surrender of it; and yet it exists not in the National Government. It is, then, a mere nonentity. Such a policy, voluntarily adopted by a free people, in subversion of some of their dearest rights and interests, would be most extraordinary in itself, without any assignable motive or reason for so great a sacrifice, and utterly without example in the history of the world. No man can doubt that domestic agriculture and manufactures may be most essentially promoted and protected by regulations of commerce. No man can doubt that it is the most usual, and generally the most efficient means of producing those results. No man can question that, in these great objects, the different States of America have as deep a stake and as vital interests as any other nation. Why, then, should the power be surrendered and annihilated? It would produce the most serious mischiefs at home, and would secure the most complete triumph over us by foreign nations. It would introduce and perpetuate national debility, if not national ruin. A foreign nation might, as a conqueror, impose upon us this restraint as a badge of dependence and a sacrifice of sovereignty, to subserve its own interests; but that we should impose it upon ourselves, is inconceivable. The achievement of our independence was almost worthless, if such a system was to be pursued. It would be in effect a perpetuation of that very system of monopoly, of encouragement of foreign manufactures, and depression of domestic industry, which was so much complained of during our colonial dependence, and which kept all America in a state of poverty and slavish devotion to British interests. Under such circumstances the Constitution would be established, not for the purposes avowed in the preamble, but for the exclusive benefit and advancement of foreign nations, to aid their manufactures and sustain their agriculture. . . . Commerce itself would ultimately be as great a sufferer by such a system as the other domestic interests. It would languish, if it did not perish. Let any man ask himself if New England or the Middle States would ever have consented to ratify a Constitution which would afford no protection to their manufactures or home industry. If the Constitution was ratified under the belief, sedulously propagated on all sides, that such protection was afforded, would it not now be a fraud upon the whole people to give a different construction to its powers?

Sec. 1085. It is idle to say that, with the consent of Congress, the States may lay duties on imports or exports, to favor their own domestic manufactures. . . . Our whole experience under the confederation established beyond all controversy the utter local futility, and even the general mischiefs of independent State legislation upon such a subject. It furnished one of the strongest grounds for the establishment of the Constitution. . . .

Sec. 1088. Besides, the power is to regulate commerce. . . .

Sec. 1089. Now, the motive of the grant of the power is not even alluded to in the Constitution. It is not even stated that Congress shall have power to promote and encourage domestic navigation and trade. A power to regulate commerce is not necessarily a power to advance its interests. It may in given cases suspend its operations and restrict its advancement and scope. Yet no man ever yet doubted the right of Congress to lay duties to promote and encourage domestic navigation, whether in the form of tonnage duties, or other preferences and privileges, either in the foreign trade, or coasting trade, or fisheries. It is as certain as anything can be, that the sole object of Congress, in securing the vast privileges to American-built ships, by such preferences, and privileges, and tonnage duties, was, to encourage the domestic manufacture of ships, and all the dependent branches of business. It speaks out in the language of all their laws, and has been as constantly avowed and acted on as any single legislative policy ever has been. No one ever dreamed that revenue constituted the slightest ingredient in these laws. They were purely for the encouragement of home manufactures, and home artisans, and home pursuits. Upon what grounds can Congress constitutionally apply the power to regulate commerce to one great class of domestic manufactures, which does not involve the right to encourage all? If it be said that navigation is a part of commerce, that is true. But a power to regulate navigation no more includes a power to encourage the manufacture of ships by tonnage duties than any other manufacture. Why not extend it to the encouragement of the growth and manufacture of cotton and hemp for sails and rigging; of timber, boards, and masts; of tar, pitch, and turpentine; of iron and wool; of sheetings and shirtings; of artisans and mechanics, however remotely connected with it? There are many products of agriculture and manufactures which are connected with the prosperity of commerce as intimately as domestic shipbuilding. If the one may be encouraged, as a primary motive in regulations of commerce, why may not the others? The truth is, that the encouragement of domestic shipbuilding is within the scope of the power to regulate commerce, simply because it is a known and ordinary means of exercising the power. It is one of many, and may be used like all others, according to legislative discretion. The motive to the exercise of a power can never form a constitutional objection to the exercise of the power.[2]

Story's most important and persuasive argument is that Congress's power to regulate commerce with foreign nations should not be so construed as to produce an obvious gap which State power cannot fill. This argument should be applied today in light of the actualities of State power when it comes to regulating and protecting the great productive businesses which seek their main outlet in interstate commerce, and which thereby involve the prosperity of the country in their prosperity. To invoke in relation to such businesses the reserved powers of the States as a ground for nullifying action by the National Government which would but for that objection lie within the sphere of national power, is a mockery, the very abandonment of the "benefits of language and intellect."

And this also was Madison's position with reference to a protective tariff. Madison did not blink the fact that such a measure produced, and was intended to produce, effects upon the internal economy of the States. He said:

Nor can the constitutional power of Congress to regulate commerce be limited to regulations operating externally only and in no manner internally, so as to interfere with, or control, the pursuits of the States. There are perhaps but few regulations of foreign com-

[2] Edition of 1851, pp. 27-37.

merce which do not operate on internal pursuits,
whether the regulations be in the form of municipal
enactments or of treaties. What is the duty which protects shipbuilding itself, which is a species of manufacture, but a regulation operating internally, and so
far inviting labor and capital from other pursuits?
What are the late stipulations in the treaty with
France, in favor of her silks and wines, but so many
interferences controlling the production of these articles among ourselves?

And further along in the same paper he stated:

The powers of government in our political system
are divided between the States in their united capacity
and in their individual capacities. The powers, taken
together, ought to be equal to all the objects of government, not specially excepted for special reasons, as
in the case of duties on exports; or not inconsistent with
the principles of republican government. The presumption, therefore, must be a violent one, that a power for
the encouragement of domestic manufactures was
meant to be included in the power vested in Congress
"to regulate commerce with foreign nations," as exercised by all nations for that purpose, unless it be left
in an adequate form with the individual States. The
question then is, whether the power has been so left
with the States; and it seems to be admitted by all,
that it has been taken from them, if not reserved to
them by the tenth section of article first of the Constitution. Now, apart from the indication on the face
of the Journal of the Federal Convention, that the
power reserved in that section was a limited one for
local purposes, it may be affirmed without hesitation,
that the States individually could not if they would,
and would not if they could, exercise it for the encouragement of their manufactures. They could not, because the imported articles being less burdened in the
other States, would find their way from and through

the adjoining States, and defeat the object; and they would not if they could, because the money accruing from the consumption of the articles would be paid, not into the State, but into the National Treasury, while the cost of guarding and enforcing the collection would exceed the advantage of the manufacture; and the advantage itself, if attained, would be, in a manner, common to all the States. The result, however, on the whole, would be, that the State making the attempt would lose the commerce in the article without gaining the manufacture of it.

The incapacity of the States separately to regulate their foreign commerce was fully illustrated by an experience which was well known to the Federal Convention when forming the Constitution. It was well known that the incapacity gave a primary and powerful impulse to the transfer of the power to a common authority capable of exercising it with effect. It may be confidently foretold, that if, as has been proposed, Congress should grant a general consent to the States to impose duties on imports in favor of their domestic manufactures, and any State should avail itself of the consent, the experiment would never be repeated by the same nor the example be followed by any other State.[3]

Not until 1927 was the question of the constitutionality of the protective tariff ever dealt with by the Supreme Court. That year, in deciding *Hampton, Jr. & Co. v. United States*,[4] Chief Justice Taft, speaking for a unanimous Court said:

The second objection to sec. 315 is that the declared plan of Congress, either expressly or by clear implication, formulates its rule to guide the President and his

[3] *Letters and Other Writings* (1867), IV, 236, 250-1.
[4] 276 U.S. 394.

advisory Tariff Commission as one directed to a tariff system of protection that will avoid damaging competition to the country's industries by the importation of goods from other countries at too low a rate to equalize foreign and domestic competition in the markets of the United States. It is contended that the only power of Congress in the levying of customs duties is to create revenue and that it is unconstitutional to frame the customs duties with any other view than that of revenue raising. It undoubtedly is true that during the political life of this country there has been much discussion between parties as to the wisdom of the policy of protection, and we may go further and say as to its constitutionality, but no historian, whatever his view of the wisdom of the policy of protection, would contend that Congress since the first Revenue Act in 1789 has not assumed that it was within its power in making provision for the collection of revenue to put taxes upon importations and to vary the subjects of such taxes or rates in an effort to encourage the growth of the industries of the nation by protecting home production against foreign competition. It is enough to point out that the second act adopted by the Congress of the United States July 4, 1789 (chap. 2, 1 Stat. at L. 24), contained the following recital:

"Sec. 1. Whereas it is necessary for the support of government, for the discharge of the debts of the United States, and the encouragement and protection of manufactures, that duties be laid on goods, wares and merchandises imported:

"Be it enacted, etc."

In this first Congress sat many members of the Constitutional Convention of 1787. This Court has repeatedly laid down the principle that a contemporaneous legislative exposition of the Constitution when the founders of our government and framers of our Constitution were actively participating in public affairs, long acquiesced in, fixes the construction to be given its provisions. *Myers v. United States*, 272 U.S. 52, 175, and cases cited. The enactment and enforcement of a number of customs revenue laws drawn with a motive of maintaining a system of protection since the Revenue Law of 1789 are matters of history.[5]

But in the more recent case of *University of Illinois v. United States*,[6] the constitutional justification of the protective tariff was transferred to the basis on which it was rested by Madison, namely to the power to regulate commerce with foreign nations. This was probably due to the fact that the Court had come to feel that there was a logical incongruity between its holding in the Hampton Case and that in the Child Labor Tax Case.[7] It is not perceived, however, that there is any less illogic in distinguishing between the power to regulate foreign and interstate commerce. The question was discussed in Chapter II *supra*.

The close relationship between production and commerce is further attested by controversies which have frequently arisen between governments with regard to the proper interpretation of the most favored nation clause of treaties; for example over the question whether the payment of bounties to selected lines of manufacture is accordant with this clause.[8]

[5] *ibid.*, 411-13.
[6] 289 U.S. 48 (1933).
[7] 259 U.S. 20 (1922).
[8] *Vd.* J. B. Moore, *International Law Digest*, V. 305-9.

2. THE PRESENT ISSUE: REGULATION OF INDUSTRY

The doctrine of the fundamental character of the distinction between production and commerce is sufficiently traced in the following dicta:

(1) MR. JUSTICE DANIEL: Commerce with foreign nations must signify commerce which in some sense is necessarily connected with these nations, transactions which either immediately, or at some stage of their progress, must be extraterritorial. The phrase can never be applied to transactions wholly internal, between citizens of the same community, or to a polity and laws whose ends and purposes and operations are restricted to the territory and soil and jurisdiction of such community. Nor can it be properly concluded, that, because the products of domestic enterprise in agriculture or manufactures, or in the arts, may ultimately become the subjects of foreign commerce, that the control of the means or the encouragements by which enterprise is fostered and protected, is legitimately within the import of the phrase foreign commerce, or fairly implied in any investiture of the power to regulate such commerce. A pretension as far-reaching as this, would extend to contracts between citizen and citizen of the same State, would control the pursuits of the planter, the grazier, the manufacturer, the mechanic, the immense operations of the collieries and mines and furnaces of the country; for there is not one of these avocations, the results of which may not become the subjects of foreign commerce, and be borne either by turnpikes, canals, or railroads, from point to point within the several States, towards an ultimate destination, like the one above mentioned. Such a pretension would effectually prevent or paralyze every effort at internal improvement by the several States;

for it cannot be supposed that the States would exhaust their capital and their credit in the construction of turnpikes, canals, and railroads, the remuneration derivable from which, and all control over which, might be immediately wrested from them, because such public works would be facilities for a commerce which, whilst availing itself of those facilities, was unquestionably internal, although intermediately or ultimately it might become foreign.[9]

(2) MR. JUSTICE LAMAR: No distinction is more popular to the common mind, or more clearly expressed in economic and political literature, than that between manufactures and commerce. Manufacture is transformation—the fashioning of raw materials into a change of form for use. The functions of commerce are different. The buying and selling and the transportation incidental thereto constitute commerce; and the regulation of commerce in the constitutional sense embraces the regulation at least of such transportation. The legal definition of the term, as given by this court in *County of Mobile v. Kimball*, 102 U.S. 691, 702 is as follows: "Commerce with foreign countries, and among the States, strictly considered, consists in intercourse and traffic, including in these terms navigation, and the transportation and transit of persons and property, as well as the purchase, sale and exchange of commodities." If it be held that the term includes the regulation of all such manufactures as are intended to be subject of commercial transactions in the future, it is impossible to deny that it would also include all productive industries that contemplate the same thing. The result would be that Congress would be invested, to the exclusion of the States, with the power to regulate, not only manufactures, but also agriculture, horticulture, stock raising, domestic fisheries, mining—in short, every branch of human industry. For is there

[9] *Veazie v. Moor*, 14 How. 567, 573-4 (1852).

one of them that does not contemplate, more or less clearly, an interstate or foreign market? Does not the wheat grower of the Northwest, and the cotton planter of the South, plant, cultivate, and harvest his crop with an eye on the prices at Liverpool, New York, and Chicago? The power being vested in Congress and denied to the States, it would follow as an inevitable result that the duty would devolve on Congress to regulate all of these delicate, multiform, and vital interests —interests which in their nature are and must be, local in all the details of their successful management.[10]

(3) MR. JUSTICE McKENNA: It [the contention] is that the products of a State that have, or are destined to have, a market in other States, are subjects of interstate commerce, though they have not moved from the place of their production or preparation.

The reach and consequences of the contention repel its acceptance. If the possibility, or, indeed, certainty of exportation of a product or article from a State determines it to be in interstate commerce before the commencement of its movement from the State, it would seem to follow that it is in such commerce from the instant of its growth or production, and in the case of coals, as they lie in the ground. The result would be curious. It would nationalize all industries, it would nationalize and withdraw from state jurisdiction and deliver to federal commercial control the fruits of California and the South, the wheat of the West and its meats, the cotton of the South, the shoes of Massachusetts and the woolen industries of other States, at the very inception of their production or growth, that is, the fruits unpicked, the cotton and wheat ungathered, hides and flesh of cattle yet "on the hoof," wool yet unshorn, and coal yet unmined, because they are in varying percentages destined for and surely to be

[10] *Kidd v. Pearson*, 128 U.S. 1, 20-1 (1888).

exported to States other than those of their production.[11]

(4) MR. JUSTICE VAN DEVANTER: Plainly the facts do not support the contention. Mining is not interstate commerce, but, like manufacturing, is a local business subject to local regulation and taxation. *Kidd v. Pearson*, 128 U.S. 1, 20: *Capital City Dairy Co. v. Ohio*, 183 U.S. 238, 246; *Delaware, Lackawanna & Western R. R. Co. v. Yurkonis*, 238 U.S. 439, 444; *Hammer v. Dagenhart*, 247 U.S. 251, 272; *United Mine Workers v. Coronado Coal Co.*, 259 U.S. 244, 410. Its character in this regard is intrinsic, is not affected by the intended use or disposal of the product, is not controlled by contractual engagements, and persists even though the business be conducted in close connection with interstate commerce. *Cornell v. Coyne*, 192 U.S. 418; *Browning v. Waycross*, 233 U.S. 16, 22; *Delaware, Lackawanna & Western R. R. Co. v. Yurkonis, supra*; *General Railway Signal Co. v. Virginia*, 246 U.S. 500, *Hammer v. Dagenhart, supra*; *Arkedelphia Milling Co. v. St. Louis Southwestern Ry. Co.*, 249 U.S. 134, 151; *Crescent Cotton Oil Co. v. Mississippi*, 257 U.S. 129, 136; *Heisler v. Thomas Colliery Co.*, 260 U.S. 245.[12]

All of these cases, however, involved simply questions of *State* power, and sustained exercises of such power against the objection that they regulated commerce among the States. In other words, the Court held that local regulation of production is not *ipso facto* a regulation of commerce among the States such as the States are forbidden to impose even in the absence of regulation by Congress.

[11] *Heisler v. Thomas Colliery Co.*, 260 U.S. 245, 259-60 (1922).
[12] *Oliver Iron Co. v. Lord*, 262 U.S. 172, 178-9 (1923).

True, in the Sugar Trust Case, where the second of the above dicta was quoted at length, an act of Congress was involved; and here the Court, in its effort to divorce commercial regulation entirely from regulation of production, committed itself, as we saw, to the enormous proposition that *any* restraint which would reach commerce from conditions attending production "would be an indirect result, *however* inevitable and whatever its extent," and would for that reason be beyond the power of Congress to remove—which is to say that in construing Congress's power over commerce among the States, when it touches productive activities, no attention should be given to facts. And this seems also to be the significance of Justice Van Devanter's assertion that the "local" quality of mining is "intrinsic" and "persists even though the business be conducted in close connection with interstate commerce." Formula alone is to rule.

For all that, since the turn of the century, the rise of large-scale industry has brought about increasing recognition of the interrelation of commerce and production and, along with this, recognition that the power which controls commerce must be able to reach production also; that the problem of effectively controlling commerce, both for its own good and the good of the nation at large, cannot be solved by morsellizing, as it were, what is in fact a continuous process; that while production and commerce are distinguishable for some purposes, they are not distinguishable when it comes to regulating them; that, in short, the issue is between *national* regulation and *no* regulation—not between national and State regulation.

An early assertion of the adequacy of national power to the situation produced by a nationalized industry is the following by Attorney General Knox, in an address given by him before the Pittsburgh Chamber of Commerce, October 14, 1903:

Is it true that although they know with growing certainty the nature of the wrong and are seeking a remedy, the Constitution as it stands does not permit them to pursue it; that amendment to that charter is first necessary; that the power of Congress does not now extend over detriments injuring the entire body of citizens in their most vital concerns because these detriments originate in the States, although the States in the aggregate, and by the cooperation which is essential, do nothing effective to remove them?

I do not believe that we find ourselves so helpless. When the currents of monopoly evil obviously flow out over State lines and cover the country, not only entering but largely filling the channels of interstate and foreign trade, it will not do to say that the evil is beyond the national reach, and that because the first step which may lead to the evil is production, which must have a fixed situs within a State, the States alone may deal with it.

If the States are a nation for some purposes, as Jefferson said, with full legislative and executive power, and exclusive regulation of interstate commerce is one of these purposes, as the Supreme Court has decided, it would seem monstrous to urge that Congress and the Executive under its authority are powerless and must sit idly by and see the channels of interstate commerce made use of to the injury of the people by monopolistic combinations.

Plainly the power must reside somewhere, either in the nation or in the States' reservations; but the effect of present doubts is to create a dilemma under which, apparently, all power vanishes, the States saying, "Some of us do and some of us do not approve or permit monopolistic production; that is our concern, but when the products cross our borders the problem passes beyond us and becomes a matter of national regulation and control"; and the nation appearing to reply, "I can deal with commerce passing beyond any one State, but effective regulation here may indirectly interfere with production, and that is a State matter which I may not touch." And so the national and local sovereignties halt and the delictum escapes. The Supreme Court has characterized the power of Congress to regulate interstate commerce, like the related and sometimes auxiliary power to tax, in terms broad and absolute; it has defined this commerce in language which is inclusive of all phases of interstate intercourse, exchange, and trade; it has merely said that production, under an initial phase of modern consolidations which primarily, at least, regards production alone, is not such commerce. I do not think it can be said that the Court has gone beyond this point. . . .

My whole purpose in what I have said is to challenge the proposition that we are hopelessly helpless under our system of government to deal with serious problems which confront us in respect to our greatest interests. Since the radical questions of human rights and human governments have been settled, the production, preservation, and distribution of wealth receive the chief attention of civilized peoples.[13]

[13] 36 *Cong. Record*, 414-15 (57th Cong., 2nd Sess.).

Two years later President Theodore Roosevelt, in his annual message of December, 1905, approached the subject of corporation control from the same angle:

The makers of our National Constitution provided especially that the regulation of interstate commerce should come within the sphere of the general government. The arguments in favor of their taking this stand were even then overwhelming. But they are far stronger today, in view of the enormous development of great business agencies, usually corporate in form. Experience has shown conclusively that it is useless to try to get any adequate regulation and supervision of these great corporations by State action. Such regulation and supervision can only be effectively exercised by a sovereign whose jurisdiction is coextensive with the field of work of the corporations—that is, by the National Government. I believe that this regulation and supervision can be obtained by the enactment of law by the Congress. If this proves impossible, it will certainly be necessary ultimately to confer in fullest form such power upon the National Government by a proper amendment of the Constitution. It would obviously be unwise to endeavor to secure such an amendment until it is certain that the result can not be obtained under the Constitution as it now is. The laws of the Congress and of the several States hitherto, as passed upon by the courts, have resulted more often in showing that the States have no power in the matter than that the National Government has power; so that there at present exists a very unfortunate condition of things, under which these great corporations doing an interstate business occupy the position of subjects without a sovereign, neither any State government nor the National Government having effective control over them. Our steady aim should be by legislation, cautiously and carefully undertaken, but resolutely persevered in, to assert the sovereignty of the National Government by affirmative action.[14]

Certain decisions of the Court, too, have recognized the unity and continuity of that series of events which, originating in an act or acts of production, comes to an end when the finished product reaches the hands of the consumer. The distinction between production and commerce in the Sugar Trust Case rests at bottom on the refusal of the Court to recognize the intent with which goods are produced, to wit, for the market, and in the case of the great industries, for the *interstate market*. In the cases just alluded to this attitude gives way to the "stream of commerce" concept. Thus speaking for the Court in *Stafford v. Wallace*,[15] in which was sustained the Packers and Stockyards Act of 1921, Chief Justice Taft said:

The object to be secured by the act is the free and unburdened flow of live stock from the ranges and farms of the West and the Southwest through the great stockyards and slaughtering centers on the borders of that region, and thence in the form of meat products to the consuming cities in the Middle West and East, or, still as live stock, to the feeding places and fattening farms in the Middle West or East for further preparation for the market. . . .

The stockyards are not a place of rest or final destination. Thousands of head of live stock arrive daily by carload and trainload lots, and must be promptly sold and disposed of and moved out to give place to the

14 Richardson, *Messages and Papers of the President*, XI, 1132-3.
15 258 U.S. 495 (1922).

constantly flowing traffic that presses behind. The stockyards are but a throat through which the current flows, and the transactions which occur therein are only incident to this current from the West to the East, and from one State to another. Such transactions can not be separated from the movement to which they contribute and necessarily take on its character. . . .

They create a local change of title, it is true, but they do not stop the flow; they merely change the private interests in the subject of the current, not interfering with, but, on the contrary, being indispensable to its continuity. The origin of the live stock is in the West, its ultimate destination known to, and intended by, all engaged in the business is in the Middle West and East either as meat products or stock for feeding and fattening. This is the definite and well understood course of business. The stockyards and the sales are necessary factors in the middle of this current of commerce.

The act, therefore, treats the various stockyards of the country as great national public utilities to promote the flow of commerce from the ranges and farms of the West to the consumers in the East. It assumes that they conduct a business affected by a public use of a national character and subject to national regulation. That it is a business within the power of regulation by legislative action needs no discussion.[16]

And in *Board of Trade v. Olsen*,[17] the same Chief Justice used similar language in sustaining the Grain Futures Act. He said:

The question of price dominates trade between the States. Sales of an article which affect the countrywide price of the article directly affect the countrywide commerce in it. By reason and authority, therefore, in

[16] *ibid.*, 514-16.
[17] 262 U.S. 1 (1923).

determining the validity of this act, we are prevented from questioning the conclusion of Congress that manipulation of the market for futures on the Chicago Board of Trade may, and from time to time does, directly burden and obstruct commerce between the States in grain, and that it recurs and is a constantly possible danger. For this reason, Congress has the power to provide the appropriate means adopted in this act by which this abuse may be restrained and avoided.[18]

And this:

Whatever amounts to more or less constant practice, and threatens to obstruct or unduly to burden the freedom of interstate commerce is within the regulatory power of Congress under the commerce clause, and it is primarily for Congress to consider and decide the fact of the danger and meet it. This Court will certainly not substitute its judgment for that of Congress in such a matter unless the relation of the subject to interstate commerce and its effect upon it are clearly non-existent.[19]

This language appears to make the question, in the case of commodities widely dealt in, whether local conditions or transactions affect interstate commerce sufficiently to warrant Congress attempting to govern them, *a question of fact which Congress itself may determine*, "unless the relation of the subject to interstate commerce and its effect upon it *are clearly non-existent*." In short, the formula on which the Sugar Trust decision was based is here superseded by the test of actuality.

[18] *ibid.*, 40.
[19] *ibid.*, 37.

Likewise, in *Lemke v. Farmers' Grain Co.*[20] the very grounds of the decision involve the inference that Congress's power over commerce carries with it at times the power to regulate production. The syllabus of the case contains the following paragraph:

In the general and usual course of its trade, a North Dakota association bought grain in that State, placed it in its elevator, loaded it promptly on cars and shipped to other States for sale. The grain, even after loading was subject to be diverted and sold locally if the price was offered, but local sales were unusual, the company's entire market, practically, being outside North Dakota. Held: (a) That the business, including the buying of the grain in North Dakota, was interstate commerce. *Dahnke-Walker Milling Co. v. Bondurant*, 257 U.S. 282. (b) As applied to this business, a North Dakota statute, c. 138, Laws 1919, requiring purchasers of grain to obtain a license and pay a license fee, and to act under a defined system of grading, inspection and weighing, and subjecting the prices paid and profits made to regulation, was a direct burden on interstate commerce.[21]

Said Justice Day in elucidation of the decision:

It is alleged that such legislation is in the interest of the grain growers and essential to protect them from fraudulent purchases, and to secure payment to them of fair prices for the grain actually sold. This may be true, but Congress is amply authorized to pass measures to protect interstate commerce if legislation of that character is needed. The supposed inconveniences and wrongs are not to be redressed by sustaining the

[20] 258 U.S. 50 (1922).
[21] *ibid.*, 55.

constitutionality of laws which clearly encroach upon the field of interstate commerce placed by the Constitution under federal control.[22]

This language necessarily implies that the protective power over producers which the decision denies the State belongs to Congress, inasmuch as the State law was disallowed in deference to Congress's power.[23]

A recent instance of judicial recognition of the intimate connection nowadays between production and commerce is the following dictum from Chief Justice Hughes' opinion for the Court in the Appalachian Coals Case:

> The interests of producers and consumers are interlinked. When industry is grievously hurt, when producing concerns fail, when unemployment mounts and communities dependent upon profitable production are prostrated, the wells of commerce go dry.[24]

The two most recent pronouncements of the Court bearing on Proposition V are its decisions in the Poultry Case (*Schechter Corp. v. United States*[25]) and *Carter v. Carter Coal Co.*,[26] in which were set aside respectively the N. I. R. A. and the Guffey Coal Conservation Act,

---

[22] *ibid.*, 60.

[23] "Though the previous cases related to State statutes only, they held these statutes void, on the ground that authority to enact them was vested exclusively in Congress, by the Constitution, which necessarily implied that when Congress did present such a statute it would be valid." Hare, *American Constitutional Law* (1888), I, 474. See also Assistant Attorney General Beck's words, quoted p. 95, *supra*.

[24] 288 U.S. 344, 372 (1933).

[25] 295 U.S. 495, decided May 27, 1935.

[26] Decided May 18, 1936.

the so-called "little N. I. R. A." The two acts were similar in claiming for Congress power under the commerce clause to regulate wages and hours in connection with productive industry in certain cases, and the Guffey Act sought also to regulate the price of soft coal when sold in interstate commerce or when sold locally in competition with such coal.

The basis of the decision in the Poultry Case, so far as the commerce clause was involved, is indicated by the following extracts from the Chief Justice's opinion for the Court:

> In determining how far the Federal Government may go in controlling intrastate transactions upon the ground that they "affect" interstate commerce, there is a necessary and well established distinction between direct and indirect effects. The precise line can be drawn only as individual cases arise, but the distinction is clear in principle. . . .

> If the commerce clause were construed to reach all enterprises and transactions which could be said to have an indirect effect upon interstate commerce, the federal authority would embrace practically all the activities of the people, and the authority of the State over its domestic concerns would exist only by sufferance of the Federal Government. Indeed, on such a theory, even the development of the State's commercial facilities would be subject to federal control.[27]

And again:

> The distinction between direct and indirect effects of intrastate transactions upon interstate commerce must be recognized as a fundamental one, essential to the maintenance of our constitutional system. Other-

[27] 295 U.S. at 546.

wise, as we have said, there would be virtually no
limit to the federal power, and for all practical purposes we should have a completely centralized government.[28]

Significant too are his summary of the Government's defense of the N. I. R. A. and his
answer to this. He reduces the former to two
main contentions.

Thus, the government argues that hours and wages
affect prices; that slaughter house men sell at a small
margin above operating costs; that labor represents 50
to 60 per cent of these costs; that a slaughterhouse
operator paying lower wages or reducing his cost by
exacting long hours of work translates his saving into
lower prices; that this results in demands for a cheaper
grade of goods; and that the cutting of prices brings
about a demoralization of the price structure. . . .
The government also makes the point that efforts to
enact state legislation establishing high labor standards
have been impeded by the belief that, unless similar
action is taken generally, commerce will be diverted
from the States adopting such standards, and that this
fear of diversion has led to demands for federal legislation on the subject of wages and hours.[29]

To the former contention he returns the
following answer:

Similar conditions may be adduced in relation to
other businesses. The argument of the government
proves too much. If the Federal Government may determine the wages and hours of employees in the internal commerce of a State, because of . . . their
indirect effect upon interstate commerce, it would
seem that a similar control might be exerted over other

[28] *ibid.*, 548.
[29] *ibid.*, 548-9.

elements of cost, also affecting prices, such as the number of employees, rents, advertising, methods of doing business, etc. All the processes of production and distribution that enter into cost could likewise be controlled. If the cost of doing an intrastate business is in itself the permitted object of federal control, the extent of the regulation or cost would be a question of discretion and not of power.[30]

And his answer to the second argument is to like effect:

The apparent implication is that the federal authority under the commerce clause should be deemed to extend to the establishment of rules to govern wages and hours in intrastate trade and industry generally throughout the country, thus overriding the authority of the States to deal with domestic problems arising from labor conditions in their internal commerce.

It is not the province of the Court to consider the economic advantages or disadvantages of such a centralized system. It is sufficient to say that the Federal Constitution does not provide for it. Our growth and development have called for wide use of the commerce power of the Federal Government in its control over the expanded activities of interstate commerce and in protecting that commerce from burdens, interferences, and conspiracies to restrain and monopolize it. But the authority of the Federal Government may not be pushed to such an extreme as to destroy the distinction, which the commerce clause itself establishes, between commerce "among the several States" and the internal concerns of the State. The same answer must be made to the contention that is based upon the serious economic situation which led to the passage of the Recovery Act—the fall in prices, the decline in

[30] *ibid.*, 549.

wages and employment, and the curtailment of the market for commodities.[31]

The decision revives, therefore, the doctrine, or rather *formula*, of the Sugar Trust Case, which classified as "indirect" and hence outside the power of Congress under the commerce clause, any effects which might reach commerce from conditions surrounding production, *"however inevitable and whatever the extent"* of such effects.

Fortunately or unfortunately, the decision was accompanied by a finding on the part of the Court that defendants' business, that of wholesale dealers in poultry, was "purely local." So the question at once arose whether the Court had intended by the above language to lay down doctrine which would be equally applicable to Congressional regulation of wages and hours in the great manufacturing and extractive industries, such as steel, coal, and so on. This question the decision in *Carter v. Carter Coal Co.* answers in the affirmative.

A salient passage from Justice Sutherland's opinion for the majority follows:

We have seen that the word "commerce" is the equivalent of the phrase "intercourse for the purposes of trade." Plainly, the incidents leading up to and culminating in the mining of coal do not constitute such intercourse. The employment of men, the fixing of their wages, hours of labor and working conditions, the bargaining in respect of these things, whether carried on separately or collectively, each and all constitute

[31] *ibid.*, 549-50.

intercourse for the purposes of production, not of trade.

The latter is a thing apart from the relation of employer and employee, which in all producing occupations is purely local in character. Extraction of coal from the mine is the aim and the completed result of local activities. Commerce in the coal mined is not brought into being by force of these activities but by negotiations, agreements and circumstances entirely apart from production. Mining brings the subject-matter of commerce into existence. Commerce disposes of it.

A consideration of the foregoing and of many cases which might be added to those already cited renders inescapable the conclusion that the effect of the labor provisions of the Act, including those in respect of minimum wages, wage agreements, collective bargaining and the labor board, and its powers, primarily falls upon production and not upon commerce, and confirms the further resulting conclusion that production is a purely local activity.

It follows that none of these essential antecedents of production constitutes a transaction in or forms any part of interstate commerce. *Schechter Corp. v. United States, supra*, p. 542 *et seq.* Everything which moves in interstate commerce has had a local origin. Without local production somewhere, interstate commerce, as now carried on, would practically disappear. Nevertheless, the local character of mining, of manufacturing and of crop-growing is a factor and remains a fact, whatever may be done with the products.[32]

And again:

Whether the effect of a given activity or condition is direct or indirect is not always easy to determine. The word "direct" implies that the activity or con-

[32] 80 Law. Ed. Advance Opinions, 749, 765-6. The case was decided May 18, 1936.

dition invoked or blamed shall operate proximately—
not mediately, remotely, or collaterally—to produce
the effect. It connotes the absence of an efficient inter-
vening agency or condition. And the extent of the effect
bears no logical relation to its character.

The distinction between a direct and an indirect
effect turns, not upon the magnitude of either the
cause or the effect, but entirely upon the manner in
which the effect has been brought about. If the production by one man of a single ton of coal intended for
interstate sale and shipment, and actually so sold and
shipped, affects interstate commerce indirectly, the
effect does not become direct by multiplying the tonnage, or increasing the number of men employed, or
adding to the expense or complexities of the business,
or by all combined.

It is quite true that rules of law are sometimes qualified by considerations of degree, as the government
argues. But the matter of degree has no bearing upon
the question here, since that question is not—what is
the extent of the local activity or condition, or the
extent of the effect produced upon interstate commerce? But—what is the relation between the activity
or condition and the effect?

Much stress is put upon the evils which come from
the struggle between employers and employees over
the matter of wages, working conditions, the right of
collective bargaining, etc., and the resulting strikes,
curtailment and irregularity of production and effect
on prices; and it is insisted that interstate commerce is
greatly affected thereby.

But, in addition to what has just been said, the conclusive answer is that the evils are all local evils over
which the Federal Government has no legislative control. The relation of employer and employee is a local
relation. At common law, it is one of the domestic relations. The wages are paid for the doing of local work.
Working conditions are obviously local conditions. The

employees are not engaged in or about commerce, but exclusively in producing a commodity. And the controversies and evils, which it is the object of the act to regulate and minimize, are local controversies and evils affecting local work undertaken to accomplish that local result. Such effect as they may have upon commerce, however extensive it may be, is secondary and indirect. An increase in the greatness of the effect adds to its importance. It does not alter its character.[33]

Obviously this language does not weaken, but rather strengthens, the inflexible character of the distinction between "direct" and "indirect" effects. "The extent of the effects bears no logical relation to its character" are Justice Sutherland's uncompromising words. The distinction is one of *kind*, not of *degree*; and this is so, his further words make it clear, because the purpose of this distinction is to maintain the States in *exclusive* possession of the power to regulate productive industry, and *especially the power to regulate the relationship of employer and employee in such industry*. Into this field of power Congress's power over commerce simply must not be construed to extend whatever may be the actual relationship in modern conditions between commerce and production.

In short, just as the primary purpose before the Civil War of the doctrine of *powers exclusively reserved to the States* was the protection of the relationship between master and slave from interference by the National Government, so its primary purpose nowadays is

[33] *ibid.*, 767-8.

to protect similarly the relationship of employer and employee, except in the case of interstate carriers. But as we saw at the close of the last chapter, the Tenth Amendment lends no support to this doctrine and the supremacy clause repels it. Whenever the National Government is *able* to interfere with "the internal concerns of a State" through the control which it can exert by virtue of its power to "regulate commerce among the several States," when these words are given their usual meanings, it is *entitled* to do so. Nor is there anything "arbitrary" about an interference of this sort which results from an act forbidding interstate commerce in goods produced for the interstate market. *Such a prohibition is effective, not as a penalty* in terrorem, *but only because of and to the extent of the actual relationship between production and interstate commerce and their reciprocal operation upon each other.*

PROPOSITION VI

PROPOSITION VI

That Congress's purpose in enacting a measure is a judicially enforcible test of the validity of such measure if it invades the ordinary domain of the States.

1. *THE PROBLEM CLARIFIED*

THE word "purpose" in the above context —or interchangeably, the word "motive" —signifies the *public advantage* which Congress seeks in enacting a measure. Proposition VI involves, therefore, in the first place, the assumption discussed in Chapter iv, that the public advantages in the promotion of which the delegated powers of Congress may be legitimately employed are relatively few, being confined for the most part to the *conservation* or *enlargement* of the subject-matter upon which they primarily operate. So far as the *major* purposes of good government the world over are concerned, the delegated powers are deemed to have been virtually sterilized, or to vary the figure, as intended to be exercised in a sort of governmental vacuum which has been pumped dry of most of the vital elements of public policy. As was pointed out earlier, this theory runs counter both to the Preamble of the Constitution and to some very positive dicta of the Court, as well as to the logical implication of several decisions.

In this chapter, however, it is a second implication of Proposition VI which is of primary interest, namely, that Congress's purposes or motives, in the sense just indicated, are subject to judicial review in protection of the reserved powers of the States. Two obstacles stand in the way of the Proposition considered from this angle. The first is the difficulty of determining motives, and especially the motives of a numerous and complex body like Congress. But formidable as this difficulty seems at first glance, the Court has a way of minimizing it by saying that the purpose of Congress may be judged by the "practical effect" of its acts. But—and this is the second difficulty—is the "practical effect" of an act of Congress so simple a matter to determine? The fact is that almost every Congressional measure inevitably gives rise to *a variety of effects*, some of which may be justifiable by the limited purpose theory, but some of which cannot be so justified.

Are we then to say that every act of Congress which in any way operates upon matters normally within the jurisdiction of the States, is void? Obviously not; we cannot repeal the history of Congressional legislation in the past, and we cannot dispense with Congressional legislation in the future. Or are we to say that the Court should attempt to weigh the various motives of Congress, and set aside those measures whose enactment appears to it to have been induced principally by the effects they were expected by Congress to produce within the ordinary domain of State power? If we do, we are again faced by difficulty no. 1, the only solution of which would then be to attribute theoretically to the Court a degree of clairvoyance which in practical operation would enable it to substitute its preferences for those of Congress *ad libitum*.

In short, if we retain Proposition VI, the only remaining choice would seem to lie between two methods of diluting the national legislative power: first, that of subordinating it to the reserved powers of the States, thus reversing the supremacy clause; or secondly, that of subordinating it to the Supreme Court endowed with an illimitable veto power. As we shall see, the Court has incurred both these dangers in the fields to which it has thus far admitted this Proposition.

2. *EARLY REJECTION OF PROPOSITION VI*

Discussing the necessary and proper clause in *McCulloch v. Maryland*, Chief Justice Marshall remarked at one point:

Should Congress, in the execution of its powers, adopt measures which are prohibited by the Constitution; or should Congress, under the pretext of executing its powers, pass laws for the accomplishment of objects not entrusted to the government; it would become the painful duty of this tribunal, should a case requiring such a decision come before it, to say that such an act was not the law of the land.[1]

This dictum is quoted in several recent opinions of the Court as if it supported Proposition VI as to both its implications.[2] Whether it does or does not depends evidently upon the meaning which Marshall attached to the word "objects" in the above context.

The dependence of Marshall for his opinion in this case upon Hamilton's opinion as to the constitutionality of the Bank of the United States, of February 23, 1791, is well known. It is therefore pertinent to collate Hamilton's use of the word "object," in the above mentioned document, for the light which it may throw upon Marshall's employment of it.

The following passages, not all of them continuous, from this document are the ones in point:

The circumstance that the powers of sovereignty are in this country divided between the National and State governments, does not afford the distinction required. It does not follow from this, that each of the portion of *powers* delegated to the one or to the other, is not sovereign with *regard to its proper objects*. It will only follow from it, that each has sovereign power as to *certain things*, and not as to *other things*.

If it would be necessary to bring proof to a proposition so clear, as that which affirms that the powers of

[1] 4 Wheat. 316, 423.
[2] 259 U.S. 20, 40; also by Justice Roberts in *United States v. Butler*, decided January 6, 1936, 80 Law. Ed. Advance Opinions, 296; and by Chief Justice Hughes in *Ashwander v. T. V. A.*, decided February 17, 1936. *ibid.*, 435.

the Federal Government, as to *its objects*, were sovereign, there is a clause of its Constitution which would be decisive.

Thus a corporation may not be erected by Congress for superintending the police of the city of Philadelphia, because they are not authorized to *regulate* the *police* of that city. But one may be erected in relation to the collection of taxes, or to the trade with foreign countries, or to the trade between the States, or with the Indian tribes; because it is the province of the Federal Government to *regulate* those objects, and because it is incident to a general *sovereign* or *legislative* power to *regulate* a thing, to employ all the means which relate to its regulation to the best and greatest advantage.

It may be truly said of every government, as well as of that of the United States, that it has only a right to pass such laws as are necessary and proper to accomplish the objects intrusted to it.

The relation between the *measure* and the *end*; between the *nature* of the *mean* employed towards the execution of a power, and the object of that power, must be the criterion of constitutionality, not the more or less of *necessity* or *utility*.

This restrictive interpretation of the word *necessary* is also contrary to this sound maxim of construction; namely, that the powers contained in a constitution of government, especially those which concern the general administration of the affairs of a country, its finances, trade, defense, etc., ought to be construed liberally in advancement of the public good. This rule does not depend on the particular form of a government, or on the particular demarkation of the boundaries of its powers, but on the nature and objects of government itself. The means by which national exigencies are to be provided for, national inconveniences obviated, national prosperity promoted, are of such infinite variety, extent, and complexity, that there must of necessity be great latitude of discretion in the selection and application of those means. Hence, consequently, the necessity and propriety of exercising the authorities intrusted to a government on principles of liberal construction.

The Attorney General admits the *rule*, but takes a distinction between a State and the Federal Constitution. The latter, he thinks, ought to be construed with greater strictness, because there is more danger of error in defining *partial* than *general* powers. But the reason of the *rule* forbids such a distinction. This reason is, the variety and extent of public exigencies, a far greater proportion of which, and of a far more critical kind, are objects of *National* than of *State* administration. The greater danger of error, as far as it is supposable, may be a prudential reason for caution in practice, but it cannot be a rule of restrictive interpretation.

But while on the one hand the construction of the Secretary of State is deemed inadmissible, it will not be contended, on the other, that the clause in question gives any *new* or *independent* power. But it gives an explicit sanction to the doctrine of *implied powers*, and is equivalent to an admission of the proposition that the government, as to its *specified powers* and *objects*, has plenary and sovereign authority, in some cases paramount to the States; in others, coordinate with it. For such is the plain import of the declaration, that it may pass all *laws* necessary and proper to carry into execution those powers.

It is no valid objection to the doctrine to say, that it is calculated to extend the power of the general government throughout the entire sphere of State legislation. The same thing has been said, and may be said, with regard to every exercise of power by *implication* or *construction*.

But the doctrine which is contended for is not chargeable with the consequences imputed to it. It does not affirm that the National Government is sovereign in all respects, but that it is sovereign to a certain extent; that is, to the extent of the objects of its specified powers.

It leaves, therefore, a criterion of what is constitutional, and of what is not so. This criterion is the *end*, to which the measure relates to a *mean*. If the *end* be clearly comprehended within any of the specified powers, and if the measure have an obvious relation to that *end*, and is not forbidden by any particular provision of the Constitution, it may safely be deemed to come within the compass of the national authority.

To this objection an answer has been already given. It is this, that the doctrine is stated with this *express qualification*, that the right to erect corporations does *only* extend to *cases* and *objects* within the *sphere* of the *specified powers* of the *government*.

It is presumed to have been satisfactorily shown in the course of the preceding observations:

1. That the power of the government, *as* to the objects intrusted to its management, is in its nature sovereign.[3]

Further light may also, conceivably, be thrown on the problem by collating certain other passages in which Marshall employed the word "object"; also the words "subject" and "purpose." Such passages follow:

All subjects over which the sovereign power of a State extends, are objects of taxation.

If, as has always been understood, the sovereignty of Congress, though limited to specified objects, is plenary as to those objects, the power over commerce with foreign nations, and among the several States, is vested in Congress as absolutely as it would be in a single government, having in its constitution the same restrictions on the exercise of the power as are found in the Constitution of the United States.

[3] *Works* (Hamilton, Ed.), IV, 105-23 *passim*.

In imposing taxes for State purposes, they are not doing what Congress is empowered to do. Congress is not empowered to tax for those purposes which are within the exclusive province of the States. When, then, each government exercises the power of taxation, neither is exercising the power of the other.

No direct general power over these objects is granted to Congress; and, consequently, they remain subject to State legislation. If the legislative power of the Union can reach them, it must be for national purposes.

So, if a State, in passing laws on subjects acknowledged to be within its control, and with a view to those subjects, shall adopt a measure of the same character with one which Congress may adopt, it does not derive its authority from the particular power which has been granted, but from some other, which remains with the State, and may be executed by the same means. All experience shows, that the same measures, or measures scarcely distinguishable from each other, may flow from distinct powers; but this does not prove that the powers themselves are identical.[4]

In the material above quoted both Hamilton and Marshall seem generally to use the word "objects" to designate either the *powers* of the National Government, or the *subject-matter* upon which these powers operate primarily. Applying this conclusion to the problem immediately under discussion, namely, the sense in which Marshall used the word "objects" on page 423 of 4 Wheaton, it strongly appears that what he had in mind to say was simply that powers exercised by Congress under the necessary and proper clause must

[4] 4 Wheat. at 429; 9 Wheat. at 197-204 *passim*.

stand in some sort of *instrumental* relationship to one or more of the express powers of the United States, and must be designed to facilitate the application of these powers to its constitutionally designated subject-matter. His use of the word "objects" instead of "powers" was apparently due to the fact that he had just used the latter word—in short, to considerations of euphony.

That Marshall clearly recognized that the ulterior purposes of general welfare for which governmental power, either State or national, may be employed are not subject to judicial inquiry, appears to follow inevitably from his assertion in *Gibbons v. Ogden* that Congress's discretion in the exercise of its power to regulate commerce, like that in declaring war, is subject only to Congress's political responsibility. This also is the conclusion logically deducible from his famous dictum that "the power to tax involves the power to destroy,"[5] as well as from his more general statement that:

Questions of power do not depend on the degree to which it may be exercised. If it may be exercised at all, it must be exercised at the will of those in whose hands it is placed. . . .

All power may be abused; and if fear of its abuse is to constitute an argument against its existence, it might be urged against the existence of that which is

[5] 4 Wheat. at 431.

universally acknowledged, and which is indispensable to the general safety.[6]

Webster voiced like doctrine in his argument in *Gibbons v. Ogden;* speaking of the monopoly there involved he said:

Now, it must be remembered, that this grant is made as an exercise of *sovereign political power*. It is not an inspection law, nor a health law, nor passed by any derivative authority; it is professedly an act of sovereign power. Of course, there is no limit to the power, to be derived from the *purpose* for which it is exercised. If exercised for one purpose, it may be also for another. No one can inquire into the motives which influence sovereign authority. It is enough, that such power manifests its will.[7]

These words bear directly upon the question of the proper relation of judicial review to legislative discretion; and such also is the case with the following section from Story's *Commentaries*, written with reference to the Calhounist argument that the protective tariff was an invasion of the powers of the States.

Sec. 1090. When an act is constitutional, as an exercise of a power, can it be unconstitutional, from the motives with which it is passed? If it can, then the constitutionality of an act must depend not upon the power, but upon the motives of the legislature. It will follow, as a consequence, that the same act passed by one legislature will be constitutional, and by another unconstitutional. Nay, it might be unconstitutional, as well from its omissions as its enactments, since if its

[6] *Brown v. Maryland*, 12 Wheat. 419, 439-40 (1827).
[7] 9 Wheat. at 23.

omissions were to favor manufactures, the motive would contaminate the whole law. Such a doctrine would be novel and absurd. It would confuse and destroy all the tests of constitutional rights and authorities. Congress could never pass any law without an inquisition into the motives of every member; and even then they might be reexaminable. Besides, what possible means can there be of making such investigations? The motives of many of the members may be, nay, must be utterly unknown, and incapable of ascertainment by any judicial or other inquiry: they may be mixed up in various manners and degrees; they may be opposite to, or wholly independent of, each other. The Constitution would thus depend upon processes utterly vague and incomprehensible; and the written intent of the legislature upon its words and acts, the *lex scripta*, would be contradicted or obliterated by conjecture, and parol declarations, and fleeting reveries, and heated imaginations. No government on earth could rest for a moment on such a foundation. It would be a constitution of sand, heaped up and dissolved by the flux and reflux of every tide of opinion. Every act of the legislature must therefore be judged of from its object and intent, as they are embodied in its provisions; and if the latter are within the scope of admitted powers, the act must be constitutional, whether the motive for it were wise or just, or otherwise. The manner of applying a power may be an abuse of it; but this does not prove that it is unconstitutional.[8]

Some of Story's objections seem rather fanciful, but they do not necessarily impair his final conclusion: "The motive to the exercise of a power can never form a constitutional objection to the exercise of the power."

[8] Edition of 1851, II, 36-7.

3. *THE NATIONAL TAXING POWER AND PROPOSITION VI*

The quotations just given from Story had reference to the definition of the power of Congress to regulate foreign commerce. But the same problem was also raised contemporaneously, and in the same connection, with reference to the national taxing power. The following passages from the *Commentaries* are apposite:

Sec. 959. First, then, as to the question, whether Congress can lay taxes, except for the purposes of revenue. . . .

Sec. 960. The argument against the constitutional authority is understood to be maintained on the following grounds, which, though applied to the protection of manufactures, are equally applicable to all other cases, where revenue is not the object. . . .

Sec. 961. It is true, that the eighth section of the first article of the Constitution authorizes Congress to lay and collect an import duty; but it is granted as a tax power, for the sole purpose of revenue; a power, in its nature, essentially different from that of imposing protective, or prohibitory duties. The two are incompatible; for the prohibitory system must end in destroying the revenue from imports. It has been said, that the system is a violation of the spirit and not of the letter of the Constitution. The distinction is not material. The Constitution may be as grossly violated by acting against its meaning, as against its letter. The Constitution grants to Congress the power of imposing a duty on imports for revenue, which power is abused by being converted into an instrument for rearing up the industry of one section of the country on the ruins of another. The violation, then, consists in using a power, granted for one object, to advance another, and that by a sacrifice of the original object. It is in a word a violation of perversion, the most dangerous of all, because the most insidious and difficult to resist. . . .

Sec. 964. The argument in favor of the constitutional authority is grounded upon the terms and the intent of the Constitution. . . .

Sec. 965. The language of the Constitution is, "Congress shall have 'power to lay and collect taxes, duties, imposts, and excises.'" If the clause had stopped here, and remained in this absolute form (as it was in fact, when reported in the first draft in the convention), there could not have been the slightest doubt on the subject. The absolute power to lay taxes, includes the power in every form in which it may be used, and for every purpose, to which the legislature may choose to apply it. This results from the very nature of such an unrestricted power. *A fortiori* it might be applied by Congress to purposes, for which nations have been accustomed to apply to it. Now, nothing is more clear, from the history of commercial nations, than the fact, that the taxing power is often, very often, applied for other purposes than revenue. It is often applied, as a regulation of commerce. It is often applied, as a virtual prohibition upon the importation of particular articles, for the encouragement and protection of domestic products, and industry; for the support of agriculture, commerce, and manufactures; for retaliation upon foreign monopolies and injurious restrictions; for mere purposes of State policy and domestic economy; sometimes to banish a noxious article of consumption; sometimes, as a bounty upon an infant manufacture, or agricultural product; sometimes, as a temporary restraint of trade; sometimes, as a suppression of particular employments; sometimes, as a prerogative power to destroy competition, and secure a monopoly to the government!

Sec. 966. If, then, the power to lay taxes, being general, may embrace, and in the practice of nations does embrace, all these objects, either separately, or in combination, upon what foundation does the argument rest, which assumes one object only, to the exclusion of all the rest? which insists, in effect, that because revenue may be one object, therefore it is the sole object of the power? which assumes its own construction to be correct, because it suits its own theory, and denies the same right to others, entertaining a different theory? If the power is general in its terms, is it not an abuse of all fair reasoning to insist that it is particular? to desert the import of the language, and to substitute other and different language? Is this allowable in regard to any instrument? Is it allowable in an especial manner, as to constitutions of government, growing out of the rights, duties, and exigencies of nations, and looking to an infinite variety of circumstances, which may require very different applications of a given power? . . .

Sec. 970. Besides; if a particular act of Congress, not for revenue, should be deemed an excess of the powers; does it follow that all other acts are so? If the common defense or general welfare can be promoted by laying taxes in any other manner than for revenue, who is at liberty to say that Congress cannot constitutionally exercise the power for such a purpose? No one has a right to say, that the common defense and general welfare can never be promoted by laying taxes, except for revenue. No one has ever yet been bold enough to assert such a proposition. Different men have entertained opposite opinions on subjects of this nature. It is a matter of theory and speculation, of political economy, and national policy, and not a matter of power. It may be wise or unwise to lay taxes, except for revenue; but the wisdom or inexpediency of a measure is no test of its constitutionality. . . .

Sec. 971. The third opinion is (as has been already stated) that the power is restricted to such specific objects, as are contained in the other enumerated powers. Now, if revenue be not the sole and exclusive means of carrying into effect all these enumerated powers, the advocates of this doctrine must maintain with those of the second opinion, that the power is not limited to purposes of revenue. No man will pretend to say, that all those enumerated powers have no other objects, or means to effectuate them, than revenue. Revenue may be one mode; but it is not the sole mode. Take the power "to regulate commerce." Is it not clear from the whole history of nations, that laying taxes is one of the most usual modes of regulating commerce? Is it not, in many cases, the best means of preventing foreign monopolies, and mischievous commercial restriction? In such cases, then, the power to lay taxes is confessedly not for revenue. If so, is not the argument irresistible, that it is not limited to purposes of revenue? Take another power, the power to coin money and regulate its value, and that of foreign coin; might not a tax be laid on certain foreign coin for the purpose of carrying this into effect by suppressing the circulation of such coin, or regulating its value? Take the power to promote the progress of science and useful arts; might not a tax be laid on foreigners, and foreign inventions, in aid of this power, so as to suppress foreign competition, or encourage domestic science and arts? Take another power, vital in the estimation of many statesmen to the security of a republic—the power to provide for organizing, arming, and disciplining the militia; may not a tax be laid on foreign arms, to encourage the domestic manufacture of arms, so as to enhance our security, and give uniformity to our organization and discipline? Take the power to declare war, and its auxiliary powers; may not Congress, for the very object of providing for the effectual exercise of these powers, and securing a permanent domestic manufacture and supply of powder, equipments, and other warlike apparatus, impose a prohibitory duty upon foreign articles of the same nature? If Congress may, in any, or all of these cases, lay taxes; then, as revenue constitutes, upon the very basis of the reasoning, no object of the taxes, is it not clear, that the enumerated powers require the power to lay taxes to be more extensively construed, than for purposes of revenue? It would be no answer to say, that the power of taxation, though in its nature only a power to raise revenue, may be resorted to, as an implied power to carry into effect these enumerated powers in any effectual manner. That would be to contend, that an express power to lay taxes is not coextensive with an *implied* power to lay taxes; that when the express power is given, it means a power to raise revenue only; but when it is implied, it no longer has any regard to this object. How then, is a case to be dealt with, of a mixed nature, where revenue is mixed up with other objects in the framing of the law?[9]

In *Veazie Bank v. Fenno*[10] an act of Congress taxing notes of issue of State banks was attacked on the ground that it was a "direct" tax and it was "so excessive as to indicate a purpose on the part of Congress to destroy" the franchises of banks affected.

[9] Ed. of 1851, I, 674-81. Mr. J. P. Jones, Princeton '36, shows in his able Senior thesis that it was taken for granted in the Convention of 1787 that the taxing power, while primarily for the raising of revenue, would be used also for purposes of regulation. Indeed, in the dispute with Great Britain leading up to the Revolution, the Colonists at one stage admitted Parliament's right to tax them for the purpose of *regulating* the trade of the Empire, but *not* for the purpose of *raising revenue*. I wish also to acknowledge the value, in connection with this chapter, of some suggestions of my young friends Mr. John A. Schroth and Mr. Benjamin R. Twiss.

[10] 8 Wall. 533 (1869).

The Court sustained the tax both as an excise and as a "necessary and proper" measure for securing a uniform currency. Thus the fact that the tax was sustainable under the currency power was not deemed to make unnecessary the vindication of the tax as one which was leviable by the rule of uniformity. In other words, *the regulatory purpose of the tax did not destroy its quality as a tax*. Furthermore, the Court said:

The judicial cannot prescribe to the legislative departments of the government limitations upon the exercise of its acknowledged powers. The power to tax may be exercised oppressively upon persons, but the responsibility of the legislature is not to the courts, but to the people by whom its members are elected. So if a particular tax bears heavily upon a corporation, or a class of corporations, it cannot, for that reason only, be pronounced contrary to the Constitution.[11]

However, in *Veazie Bank v. Fenno* the regulation effected by the tax operated within an acknowledged field of national jurisdiction. In *McCray v. United States*,[12] the contrary was the case. Here the act under review imposed a tax of ten cents per pound on oleomargarine colored to resemble butter. The tax was assailed on the ground that it was so heavy that it was evidently imposed "not as an excise for revenue, but as a prohibition," and that in this respect it operated "to regulate the interior commerce of the States, which was ex-

[11] *ibid.*, 548-9.
[12] 195 U.S. 27 (1904).

pressly reserved to the States by the Tenth Amendment." The Court, speaking by Justice White, sustained the tax. Relevant passages from his opinion are the following:

Whilst, as a result of our written Constitution, it is axiomatic that the judicial department of the government is charged with the solemn duty of enforcing the Constitution, and therefore in cases properly presented, of determining whether a given manifestation of authority has exceeded the power conferred by that instrument, no instance is afforded from the foundation of the government where an act, which was within a power conferred, was declared to be repugnant to the Constitution, because it appeared to the judicial mind that the particular exertion of constitutional power was either unwise or unjust. To announce such a principle would amount to declaring that in our constitutional system the judiciary was not only charged with the duty of upholding the Constitution but also with the responsibility of correcting every possible abuse arising from the exercise by the other departments of their conceded authority. So to hold would be to overthrow the entire distinction between the legislative, judicial and executive departments of the government upon which our system is founded, and would be a mere act of judicial usurpation.

It is, however, argued if a lawful power may be exerted for an unlawful purpose, and thus by abusing the power it may be made to accomplish a result not intended by the Constitution, all limitations of power must disappear, and the grave function lodged in the judiciary, to confine all the departments within the authority conferred by the Constitution, will be of no avail. This, when reduced to its last analysis, comes to this, that, because a particular department of the government may exert its lawful powers with the object or motive of reaching an end not justified, therefore it becomes the duty of the judiciary to restrain the exercise of a lawful power wherever it seems to the judicial mind that such lawful power has been abused. But this reduces itself to the contention that, under our constitutional system, the abuse by one department of the government of its lawful powers is to be corrected by the abuse of its powers by another department.

The proposition, if sustained, would destroy all distinction between the powers of the respective departments of the government, would put an end to that confidence and respect for each other which it was the purpose of the Constitution to uphold, and would thus be full of danger to the permanence of our institutions. . . .

It is, of course, true, as suggested, that if there be no authority in the judiciary to restrain a lawful exercise of power by another department of the government, where a wrong motive or purpose has impelled to the exertion of the power, that abuses of a power conferred may be temporarily effectual. The remedy for this, however, lies, not in the abuse by the judicial authority of its functions, but in the people, upon whom, after all, under our institutions, reliance must be placed for the correction of abuses committed in the exercise of lawful power. . . .

The decisions of this Court from the beginning lend no support whatever to the assumption that the judiciary may restrain the exercise of lawful power on the assumption that a wrongful purpose or motive has caused the power to be exerted. . . .[13]

Forced to choose between his conception of Dual Federalism and his conception of the Separation of Powers, Justice White adhered to the latter.

---

[13] *ibid.*, 54-6. Cf. Chief Justice Marshall's similar attitude in a case in which the "purpose" doctrine would have come in extremely handy. *Providence Bank v. Billings*, 5 Pet. 514, 563 (1830).

Foiled by the decision in *Hammer v. Dagen-hart*, the opponents of child labor sought next to attain their objective by levying a special tax on the incomes of concerns employing such labor. The validity of this tax furnished the issue of the Child Labor Tax Case.[14] The Brief for the government by Solicitor General Beck contained the following interesting observations respecting the proper limits of judicial review:

Under our dual form of government, it is inevitable that there should be conflicting incidences of laws. Thus in the most difficult of our problems—the problem of distributing the power over commerce between interstate and intrastate commerce—it is inevitable that all State commercial regulations have an incidental effect upon interstate commerce, and that all Federal trade regulations have an incidental effect upon intrastate commerce.

So, too, it is inevitable that, when the Federal Government exercises its comprehensive power to tax, the incidences of the tax must often affect subjects which are within the reserved rights of the States. An attempt to avert this is as futile as Mrs. Partington's attempt to sweep up the Atlantic Ocean with a mop and broom.

As a result, there are many laws—Federal and State—which are *politically anticonstitutional*, without being *juridically unconstitutional*.

This distinction may be imperfectly grasped by the general public. The impression is general—and I believe that it is a mischievous one—that the judiciary has an unlimited power to nullify a law if its incidental effect is in excess of the governmental sphere of the enacting body. Our whole constitutional jurisprudence,

[14] *Bailey v. Drexel Furniture Co.*, 259 U.S. 20 (1922).

with respect to the dual power over commerce, shows that this is not the fact.

Moreover, there is a large field of political action, into which the judiciary may not enter. It is the sphere of action which may be described as that of political discretion. The motives and objectives of an exercise of a delegated power are always matters of political discretion. . . .

Therefore the only question can be, when the validity of a law is under question:

Is such a law *in its field of operation* within the delegated power of Congress? The motives of Congress and the incidence of the law are beyond judicial censorship. . . .

Congress may pass many laws within the scope of its powers, and yet the real motive or objective of the laws may be the accomplishment of a design which is equally in excess of its true functions and plainly an attempt, by indirection, to accomplish an unconstitutional end.

This is deplorable. It is anticonstitutional. It may be subversive of our form of government; but, here again, the only remedy is with the people.

If the judiciary attempts to impugn the motives and objectives of a coordinate branch of the government, whether it be executive or legislative, it attempts a futile and impossible task.

In the first place, the motives and objectives are, in nearly all cases, a matter of conjecture. To impute a wrongful motive, where there may be a rightful one, is an intolerable impeachment by one branch of the government of the work of another. In the case of the executive, the motive or objective may be in a single brain and may be gathered by his declarations; but in the case of the legislature, the judiciary is dealing with a hydra-headed body, and when Congress passes a law it is impossible to determine what motives influenced the various members of the legislature, or even a majority thereof.

Apart from the futility of the inquiry, however plausible a conjecture may be, there remains a far graver consideration that, while the human mind is what it is, it is impossible to prevent officials, in discharging their duties, from taking into account motives and objectives of a political nature. . . .

Applying these considerations to the instant case, I argue that, however plausible the conjecture, this Court is powerless to say judicially that the motives of Congress in levying the tax under consideration was not to impose a tax, but to regulate child labor; and I further argue that, even if it were, that the fact remains that if, in levying the tax upon manufacturers that employ child labor, it did so with a recognition that such a tax might result in no revenue at all, and virtually prohibit the employment of child labor, that such purpose, while it may be *politically anticonstitutional*, in the sense that it may indirectly and incidentally regulate a matter otherwise within the discretion of the States, yet it is not *juridically unconstitutional*, because it is an exercise of an undoubted power to impose a tax; and the motives and objectives of the tax are within that broad field of political discretion into which the judiciary is powerless to enter. To use Madison's phrase, it is an "extra-judicial" question and as such beyond the power of the Court.

I recognize that this doctrine, carried to its logical conclusion, could, if Congress should utilize all its great powers to accomplish ulterior ends, go far to subvert our form of government. To that possibility I can not be blind; but, nevertheless, the remedy is not with the judiciary, but with the people.

The belief that the judiciary is fully empowered to sit in judgment upon the motives or objectives of other branches of the government is a mischievous one, in that it so lowers the sense of constitutional morality among the people that neither in the legislative branch of the government nor among the people is there as strong a purpose as formerly to maintain their constitutional form of government.

Let this Court clearly say that in this broad field of political discretion there is no revisory power in the judiciary, and that the remedy must lie in the people, then, if there be any longer a sufficient sense of constitutional morality in this country, the people will themselves protect their Constitution.

The erroneous idea that this Court is the sole guardian and protector of our constitutional form of government has inevitably led to an impairment, both with the people and with their representatives, of what may be called the constitutional conscience.[15]

This proved too strong doctrine for the Court. Not only had Congress threatened the principle of dualism, but it had challenged the authority of the Court itself by seeking to circumvent it. The following paragraphs from Chief Justice Taft's opinion for the Court are the pivotal ones:

It is the high duty and function of this Court in cases regularly brought to its bar to decline to recognize or enforce seeming laws of Congress, dealing with subjects not entrusted to Congress but left or committed by the supreme law of the land to the control of the States. We can not avoid the duty even though it requires us to refuse to give effect to legislation designed to promote the highest good. The good sought in unconstitutional legislation is an insidious feature because it leads citizens and legislators of good purpose to promote it without thought of the serious breach it will make in the ark of our covenant or the harm which

[15] Brief cited, 46-54. *Cf.* the brief in 259 U.S., 21-8.

will come from breaking down recognized standards. In the maintenance of local self-government on the one hand, and the national power, on the other, our country has been able to endure and prosper for near a century and a half.

Out of a proper respect for the acts of a coordinate branch of the government, this Court has gone far to sustain taxing acts as such, even though there has been ground for suspecting from the weight of the tax it was intended to destroy its subject. But, in the act before us, the presumption of validity cannot prevail, because the proof of the contrary is found on the very face of its provisions. Grant the validity of this law, and all that Congress would need to do, hereafter, in seeking to take over to its control any one of the great number of subjects of public interest, jurisdiction of which the States have never parted with, and which are reserved to them by the Tenth Amendment, would be to enact a detailed measure of complete regulation of the subject and enforce it by a so-called tax upon departures from it. To give such magic to the word "tax" would be to break down all constitutional limitation of the powers of Congress and completely wipe out the sovereignty of the States.[16]

In the recent case of *Magnano Co. v. Hamilton*,[17] which concerned a tax closely resembling that sustained in the McCray Case, the Court again reiterated that the mere burdensomeness of a tax did not suffice to invalidate it. On the other hand, the decision in *United States v. Constantine* during the current term indicates that a majority of the present Court regards the Child Labor Tax Case as still good

[16] 259 U.S. at 37-8.
[17] 292 U.S. 40 (1934).

law.[18] In the Constantine Case a section of the Revenue Act of 1926 which levied a special excise tax of $1,000 upon a liquor dealer conducting a business contrary to the law of the State was held void as being "in the nature of a penalty for violation of State law, rather than a tax," and hence "an invasion of the police power inherent in the States."

Justice Cardozo, speaking also for Justices Brandeis and Stone dissented, saying:

The judgment of the Court, if I interpret the reasoning aright, does not rest upon a ruling that Congress would have gone beyond its power if the purpose that it professed was the purpose truly cherished. The judgment of the Court rests upon the ruling that another purpose, not professed, may be read beneath the surface, and by the purpose so imputed the statute is destroyed. Thus the process of psychoanalysis has spread to unaccustomed fields. There is a wise and ancient doctrine that a court will not inquire into the motives of a legislative body or assume them to be wrongful. *Fletcher v. Peck*, 6 Cranch, 87, 130; *Magnano Co. v. Hamilton,* 292 U.S. 40, 44.[19]

In short, the Court today accepts Proposition VI to some indefinite extent as a protection of the reserved powers of the States against the national taxing power. The cases assert that neither the burdensomeness of a tax nor its failure to produce revenue is sufficient to authorize judicial disallowance of it.

[18] Decided December 9, 1935, 80 Law. Ed. Advance Opinions, 195. See also Justice Roberts's language in *United States v. Butler, ibid.,* 298.

[19] 80 Law. Ed. Advance Opinions, 201.

There must be other stigmata of unconstitutional purpose; but whether these have to
appear on "the face of the Act" or "may be
read beneath the surface," the Constantine
Case, in the judgment of three Justices, leaves
uncertain. Perhaps we should say that the test
of constitutionality stated in Proposition VI
is today established in the field of the national
taxing power in the sense that the Court is
free to invoke it and equally free not to invoke
it, pretty much as it pleases. In the former
case the tax is a "penalty," in the latter it is a
"tax."

4. *PROPOSITION VI OUTSIDE THE FIELD OF TAXATION*

In certain other fields of national power the
Court has repeatedly disavowed Proposition
VI in recent years.

In *Weber v. Freed*[20] the Court, had before it
the Act of July 31, 1912, making it unlawful

> To bring or to cause to be brought into the United
> States from abroad, any film or other pictorial repre-
> sentation of any prize fight or encounter of pugilists,
> under whatever name, which is designed to be used or
> may be used for purposes of public exhibition.

The argument against the act was stated by
Chief Justice White as follows:

> The ground relied on for the relief was the averment
> that the prohibition of the act of Congress in question
> was repugnant to the Constitution because in enacting
> the same "Congress exceeded its designated powers

[20] 239 U.S. 325 (1915).

under the Constitution of the United States and attempted, under the guise of its powers under the Commerce Clause, to exercise police power expressly
reserved in the States."[21]

This argument was answered by the Chief
Justice, in part as follows:

The proposition plainly is wanting in merit, since it
rests upon the erroneous assumption that the motive
of Congress in exerting its plenary power may be taken
into view for the purpose of refusing to give effect to
such power when exercised. *Doyle v. Continental Ins.
Co.*, 94 U.S. 535, 541; *McCray v. United States*, 195
U.S. 27, 53-9; *Calder v. Michigan*, 218 U.S. 591, 598.[22]

In *Hamilton v. Kentucky Distilleries*,[23] a
similar argument against War Prohibition was
met by the Court, speaking by Justice Brandeis, in the following terms:

No principle of our constitutional law is more firmly
established than that this Court may not, in passing
upon the validity of a statute, enquire into the motives
of Congress. *United States v. Des Moines Navigation
Co.*, 142 U.S. 510, 544; *McCray v. United States*, 195
U.S. 27, 53-9; *Weber v. Freed*, 239 U.S. 325, 330;
Dakota Central Telephone Co. v. South Dakota, 250
U.S. 163, 184. Nor may the Court enquire into the
wisdom of the legislation. *McCulloch v. Maryland*, 4
Wheat. 316, 421; *Gibbons v. Ogden*, 9 Wheat. 1, 197;
Brushaber v. Union Pacific R. R. Co., 240 U.S. 1, 25;
Rast v. Van Deman & Lewis Co., 240 U.S. 342, 357. Nor
may it pass upon the necessity for the exercise of a
power possessed, since the possible abuse of a power is

[21] *ibid.*, 328-9.
[22] *ibid.*, 329.
[23] 251 U.S. 146 (1919).

not an argument against its existence. *Lottery Case*, 188 U.S. 321, 363.[24]

And it was also Justice Brandeis who spoke for the Court in *Arizona v. California*,[25] in which the constitutionality of the Boulder Dam project was assailed on the ground that it was not a bona fide scheme for the improvement of navigation but was intended to promote other interests not within national power. Justice Brandeis answered this argument as follows:

Into the motives which induced members of Congress to enact the Boulder Canyon Project Act, this Court may not enquire. *McCray v. United States*, 195 U.S. 27, 53-9, 49 L. ed. 78, 94-7, 24 Sup. Ct. 769, 1 Ann. Cas. 561; *Weber v. Freed*, 239 U.S. 325, 329, 330. . . .
The fact that purposes other than navigation will also be served could not invalidate the exercise of the authority conferred, even if those other purposes would not alone have justified an exercise of congressional power. Compare *Veazie Bank v. Fenno*, 8 Wall. 533, 548. . . .
It is urged that the Court is not bound by the recital of purposes in the act; that we should determine the purpose from its probable effect; and that the effect of the project will be to take out of the river, now non-navigable through lack of water, the last half of its remaining average flow. But the act specifies that the dam shall be used: "First, for river regulation, improvement of navigation and flood control; second, for irrigation and domestic uses and satisfaction of present perfected rights . . . and third, for power." It is

[24] *ibid.*, 161-2.
[25] 283 U.S. 423 (1931).

true that the authority conferred is stated to be "subject to the Colorado River Compact," and that instrument makes the improvement of navigation subservient to all other purposes. But the specific statement of primary purpose in the act governs the general references to the compact. This Court may not assume that Congress had no purpose to aid navigation, and that its real intention was that the stored water shall be so used as to defeat the declared primary purpose. Moreover, unless and until the stored water, which will consist largely of flood waters now wasted, is consumed in new irrigation projects or in domestic use, substantially all of it will be available for the improvement of navigation. The possible abuse of the power to regulate navigation is not an argument against its existence. *Lottery Case (Champion v. Ames)* 188 U.S. 321, 363.[26]

In the recent case of *Ashwander v. Tennessee Valley Authority*[27] the Chief Justice's analysis of the constitutional issues presented eliminated from judicial consideration all questions respecting the purposes or motives of the national authorities.

That, on the other hand, Proposition VI was a factor of the result reached by the Court in *Hammer v. Dagenhart* is made evident by Justice Holmes in his dissenting opinion; as well as by Chief Justice Taft's comment on the case in his opinion for the Court in the Child Labor Tax Case which was quoted in Chapter IV.[28]

[26] *ibid.*, 455-7.
[27] *Vd.* note 2, *supra.*
[28] *Vd.* p. 106, *supra.* The Court seems to have manipulated the "purpose" test first in the case of State legislation affecting inter-

The most recent case in which Proposition VI was invoked by the Court is *United States v. Butler*,[29] in which the A. A. A. was set aside as not a constitutional exercise of the national taxing-spending power but an invasion of the reserved power of the States to regulate agricultural production. Here indeed, the test is, to all appearance, applied in a form that would totally repeal the supremacy clause so far as the spending power is concerned, and this in face of the fact that Justice Roberts, who spoke for the Court, took occasion to announce its acceptance of the Hamiltonian broad view of that power!

The core of Justice Roberts's argument consists of the following passage from his opinion for the Court:

From the accepted doctrine that the United States is a government of delegated powers, it follows that those not expressly granted, or reasonably to be implied from such as are conferred, are reserved to the States or to the people. To forestall any suggestion to the contrary, the Tenth Amendment was adopted. The same proposition otherwise stated, is that powers not granted are prohibited. None to regulate agricultural production is given, and therefore legislation by Congress for that purpose is forbidden.

state commerce. For a defense of this practice, see Louis M. Greeley, "Test of a Regulation of Interstate Commerce," 1 *Harv. L. R.*, 159-84. As Mr. Greeley shows, the "purpose" test is implied in the dicta of several of the Justices in both the License and the Passenger Cases. See also the article by Professor Theodore W. Cousens, "The Use of the Federal Interstate Commerce Power to Regulate Matters within the States," 21 *Va. L. R.* (November 1934), 51-75.

[29] *Vd.* note 2, *supra*.

It is an established principle that the attainment of a prohibited end may not be accomplished under the pretext of the exertion of powers which are granted.[30]

This is all very ingenious, but cannot be allowed. To say that the National Government has not a specifically delegated power to regulate agriculture is one thing; to say that it may never so exercise any of its delegated powers as to regulate agriculture whether indirectly, or as in war time directly, is quite another thing, *unless and until it is shown that the regulation of agriculture is exclusively appropriated to powers not delegated to the National Government*.

Justice Roberts's argument boils down therefore to the proposition that the delegated powers of the United States imply certain *relatively limited ends and no others*. What are these? In view of the decision in the instant case, his thought seems to be that if it is within the reserved powers of the States to do something on a *local* scale, the National Government is not permitted to attempt a comparable end on a *more general* scale.

And this inference is borne out by his reference to agricultural conditions:

It does not help to declare that local conditions throughout the nation have created a situation of national concern; for this is but to say that whenever there is a widespread similarity of local conditions, Congress may ignore constitutional limitations upon

[30] 80 Law. Ed. Advance Opinions, 296.

its own powers and usurp those reserved to the States. . . .[31]

This should be answered by saying that "it does not help" to describe a widespread condition, which is due to general causes, which affects the prosperity of the entire country, and with which the reserved powers of the States are obviously unable to deal, as "a widespread similarity of local conditions." So to do is merely to substitute words for actualities.

Justice Roberts concludes his opinion with what Professor Powell has well termed "a parade of horribles." He says:

Should Congress ascertain that sugar refiners are not receiving a fair profit, and that this is detrimental to the entire industry, and in turn has its repercussions in trade and commerce generally, it might, in analogy to the present law, impose an excise of two cents a

[31] 80 Law. Ed. Advance Opinions, 299. At certain places Justice Roberts seems to be endeavoring to avoid the criticism that he is subordinating a delegated power of the United States to the reserved powers of the States by indicating a conception of the spending power which would adjust it to the reserved powers, but his efforts in this direction involve giving ordinary words such extraordinary meanings that they can hardly be considered persuasive. When the government, we are told, required agriculturists to sign certain contracts as a condition to their receiving certain payments from the Treasury, it "coerced" the agriculturists, who "involuntarily" accepted its terms. (80 Law. Ed. Advance Opinions, 297-9.) Had, however, Mr. Henry Ford stood in the place of the government in such a transaction, it is very doubtful indeed whether Justice Roberts would have used such terms to describe it. As a matter of fact, there are still cases in good standing which hold that a laborer is not "coerced" who has been confronted by his employer with the alternative of giving up his job or quitting his union. (*Coppage v. Kansas*, 236 U.S. 1, and cases there cited.) Apparently Justice Roberts thinks agriculturists are a very tender-minded folk, and need a special degree of protection from the Court.

pound on every sale of the commodity and pass the funds collected to such refiners, and such only, as will agree to maintain a certain price.

Assume that too many shoes are being manufactured throughout the nation; that the market is saturated, the price depressed, the factories running half-time, the employees suffering. Upon the principle of the statute in question Congress might authorize the Secretary of Commerce to enter into contracts with shoe manufacturers providing that each shall reduce his output and that the United States will pay him a fixed sum proportioned to such reduction, the money to make the payments to be raised by a tax on all retail shoe dealers or their customers.

Suppose that there are too many garment workers in large cities; that this results in dislocation of the economic balance. Upon the principle contended for an excise might be laid on the manufacture of all garments manufactured and the proceeds paid to those manufacturers who agree to remove their plants to cities having not more than a hundred thousand population. Thus, through the asserted power of taxation, the Federal Government, against the will of individual States, might completely redistribute the industrial population.

A possible result of sustaining the claimed federal power would be that every business group which thought itself underprivileged might demand that a tax be laid on its vendors or vendees the proceeds to be appropriated to the redress of its deficiency of income.

These illustrations are given, not to suggest that any of the purposes mentioned are unworthy, but to demonstrate the scope of the principle for which the government contends; to test the principle by its applications; to point out that, by the exercise of the asserted power, Congress would, in effect, under the pretext of exercising the taxing power, in reality accomplish prohibited ends. It cannot be said that they envisage improbable legislation. The supposed cases are no more improbable than would the present act have been deemed a few years ago.

Until recently no suggestion of the existence of any such power in the Federal Government has been advanced. The expressions of the framers of the Constitution, the decisions of this Court interpreting that instrument and the writings of great commentators will be searched in vain for any suggestion that there exists in the clause under discussion or elsewhere in the Constitution, the authority whereby every provision and every fair implication from that instrument may be subverted, the independence of the individual States obliterated, and the United States converted into a central government exercising uncontrolled police power in every State of the Union, superseding all local control or regulation of the affairs or concerns of the States.

Hamilton himself, the leading advocate of broad interpretation of the power to tax and to appropriate for the general welfare, never suggested that any power granted by the Constitution could be used for the destruction of local self-government in the States. Story countenances no such doctrine. It seems never to have occurred to them, or to those who have agreed with them, that the general welfare of the United States (which has aptly been termed "an indestructible Union, composed of indestructible States") might be served by obliterating the constituent members of the Union. But to this fatal conclusion the doctrine contended for would inevitably lead. And its sole premise is that though the makers of the Constitution, in erecting the Federal Government, intended sedulously to limit and define its powers, so as to reserve to the States and the people sovereign power, to be wielded by the States and their citizens and not to be invaded by the United States, they nevertheless by a single clause gave power to the Congress to tear down the barriers, to invade the States' jurisdiction, and to become a parliament of the whole people, subject to no restrictions save such as are self-imposed. The argument when seen in its true character and in the light of its inevitable results must be rejected.[32]

To this line of reasoning Justice Stone, speaking for himself and Justices Brandeis and Cardozo, answered as follows:

That the governmental power of the purse is a great one is not now for the first time announced. Every student of the history of government and economics is aware of its magnitude and of its existence in every civilized government. Both were well understood by the framers of the Constitution when they sanctioned the grant of the spending power to the Federal Government, and both were recognized by Hamilton and Story, whose views of the spending power as standing on a parity with the other powers specifically granted, have hitherto been generally accepted.

The suggestion that it must now be curtailed by judicial fiat because it may be abused by unwise use hardly rises to the dignity of argument. So may judicial power be abused. "The power to tax is the power to destroy," but we do not, for that reason, doubt its existence, or hold that its efficacy is to be restricted by its incidental or collateral effects upon the States. See *Veazie Bank v. Fenno*, 8 Wall. 533; *McCray v. United States*, 195 U.S. 27, compare *A. Magnano Co. v. Hamilton*, 292 U.S. 40. The power to tax and spend is not without constitutional restraints. One restriction is that the purpose must be truly national. Another is that it may not be used to coerce action left to State control. Another is the conscience and patriotism of Congress and the Executive. "It must be remembered that

[32] 80 Law. Ed. Advance Opinions, 300-1.

legislators are the ultimate guardians of the liberties and welfare of the people in quite as great a degree as the Courts." Justice Holmes in *Missouri, K. & T. R. Co. v. May*, 194 U.S. 267, 270.

A tortured construction of the Constitution is not to be justified by recourse to extreme examples of reckless Congressional spending which might occur if courts could not prevent expenditures which, even if they could be thought to effect any national purpose, would be possible only by action of a legislature lost to all sense of public responsibility. Such suppositions are addressed to the mind accustomed to believe that it is the business of courts to sit in judgment on the wisdom of legislative action. Courts are not the only agency of government that must be assumed to have capacity to govern. Congress and the courts both unhappily may falter or be mistaken in the performance of their constitutional duty. But interpretation of our great charter of government which proceeds on any assumption that the responsibility for the preservation of our institutions is the exclusive concern of any one of the three branches of government, or that it alone can save them from destruction is far more likely, in the long run, "to obliterate the constituent members" of "an indestructible union of indestructible states" than the frank recognition that language, even of a constitution, may mean what it says: that the power to tax and spend includes the power to relieve a nationwide economic maladjustment by conditional gifts of money.[33]

The issue between Justices Roberts and Stone is, in essence, that of the soundness of Proposition VI. Justice Stone holds that the Court may not interfere with results which Congress is able to achieve in the exercise of its

[33] *ibid.*, 306.

powers when these are defined by giving the words in which they are granted by the Constitution their usual meanings. Justice Roberts holds, on the other hand, that the Court has a higher mission when it sees an act of Congress invading the usual domain of the States, namely, that of coming—at discretion —to the rescue of the federal system. Justice Stone has the obvious advantage that the Constitution delegates the powers of Congress in black and white and endows them with supremacy over conflicting State laws in the same clear-cut fashion, whereas Justice Roberts's federal system is to a great extent an importation into our Constitutional Law of outside theorizing. Justice Stone stands by the Constitutional Document; Justice Roberts stands by a judicial gloss upon it, some of which is of his own immediate fabrication.[34]

[34] A cognate issue is admirably put in the following words from Assistant Attorney General Dickinson's argument in *Carter v. Carter Coal Co.*:

"No one would deny that dualism is a fundamental principle of the Constitution. There can be no doubt that ours is a dual system of government, certain powers being conferred upon the Federal Government and others reserved to the States. But I submit that the question of what that dualism means, in respect of any particular power, and whether, under the dual system, a particular power belongs to the Federal Government, on the one hand, or to the States, on the other hand, is not to be determined by resorting from the obscure to the more obscure, and by appealing to a vague general descriptive abstract word like dualism, but is to be determined rather by the express language of the Constitution itself, and that it does not justify an appeal from the specific language of the Constitution to an extraneous and descriptive abstraction which is nothing more than a generalized and therefore incomplete statement about what the instrument is supposed to contain. . . .

"Our Government is a dual government only because the Constitution makes it so, and it is a dual government only to the extent and in the way in which the Constitution makes it so; and if we look to the Constitution we find that it has conferred on the Federal Government—subject, of course, to other express provisions of the Constitution—the power to regulate interstate commerce with all that that implies." Senate Doc. No. 197, 74th Cong., 2nd Sess., pp. 11-12.

CHAPTER EIGHT

CONCLUSIONS

CONCLUSIONS

W HAT are we to say, in summary, of the theory of the commerce power set forth or implied in the six Propositions discussed in the preceding chapters? Three things may be said of it: first, that it has no logical basis in the Constitution itself; secondly, that its historical foundations are about equally shaky; thirdly, that its standing even in the decisions of the last forty years, the era of *laissez faire*-ism on the Bench, is equivocal, that it is open to challenge and contradiction from many decisions of the same period.

Madison's assertion in his letter to Cabell, forty years after the Constitution went into effect and after Madison himself had boxed the compass of opinion regarding the nature of the Union and the powers of the National Government—not to mention a number of other subjects—falls of its own logical absurdity. The framers of the Constitution had a fair command of the English language; and at any rate it is incredible that, if they did not mean to confer power on the National Government for its own "positive purposes" over commerce among the States, they should have used the very expression which they must have used—and which, with reference to foreign commerce, they *did* use—had they entertained that intention.

Nor is it conceivable that the verb "regulate," which occurs *once* in the commerce clause, first grants power to the National Government; then merely withdraws power from the States, which are not mentioned; then again grants power to the National Government, namely, over commerce with the Indian tribes. What the clause does, *literally and precisely*, is to grant power to Congress *to regulate commerce*, which commerce is then classified into the three branches of foreign, among the States, and with the Indian tribes. With reference, however, to each of these branches *it is one and the same power*; and that the power to regulate commerce among the States is of equal scope with the power to regulate foreign commerce was asserted by the Court again and again prior to 1900.

The idea that the power to regulate commerce does not include the power to prohibit it rests on foundations equally flimsy. As Justice Holmes pointed out in his dissent in *Hammer v. Dagenhart*, all regulation necessarily involves prohibition—if the regulation is not complied with, prohibition follows. Furthermore, the opinion of the Court in the same case admits that there are cases in which prohibition is desirable for the avoidance of "harmful results." But if this is so, then who is the judge, if not the body to which the power

to regulate is committed? Furthermore, as was
pointed out in Chapter III, the idea most immediately associated with the word "regulate"
in 1787 and long afterward was the idea of
restraint, prohibition, monopoly. It was only at
a later date that the notion of *promoting* and
fostering commerce came to be extensively
associated with the commerce power. Nor was
Proposition II first advanced with reference to
the power over *interstate* commerce, but with
reference to the power over *foreign* commerce,
in connection with Jefferson's Embargo. Not
till 1841 was a similar idea broached as to the
former power as an outgrowth of the contemporary anxieties of slavery.

As a matter of fact, no one would seriously
contend today for Proposition II, even in the
attenuated form of Proposition III. In short,
the theory that the word "regulate," carries
with it some inherent deficiency capable of
limiting the power of Congress over commerce
among the States may be regarded as today
largely abandoned. At the same time, nevertheless, it is insisted that the coexistence of
State power imposes an *extrinsic* limitation on
this power—Propositions IV and V.

A logical interpretation of the relevant provisions of the Constitution clearly and un-
avoidably forbids the idea that the reserved
powers of the States comprise an independent
limitation upon the delegated powers of the
National Government. By the terms of the

Tenth Amendment if a power is delegated to the United States by the Constitution, it is *not* reserved to the States; and by the supremacy clause, an act of Congress passed by virtue of a delegated power or powers of the United States is supreme over all conflicting State laws and constitutional provisions without exception. Obviously, powers which, when exercised, are subject to be overridden by other powers, cannot set a limit to the latter; and certainly if a State possesses a power it may exercise it. It is apparent that a reserved power of a State cannot be more potent when dormant to limit the delegated powers of the United States than when it is exercised. Nor does the Tenth Amendment recognize "fields" or "subjects" or "concerns" which it reserves to the States; it speaks *only* of "powers."

The attempt to set up the reserved powers of the States as an independent limitation upon the delegated powers of the United States is neither more nor less than a proposal to destroy the most vital single provision of the Constitution—the supremacy clause —in the guise of construing the Constitution. The truth is, that nobody since Calhoun has ever had the audacity to suggest that *all* the reserved powers of the States set a limit to the delegated powers of the United States, and even he endeavored to veil his contention with a construction of the necessary and proper clause which made conflict with the reserved powers a test of the *propriety* of an act of Congress. On the other hand, the Tenth Amendment recognizes no distinction between reserved powers which are capable of setting a limit to national power and reserved powers of lesser degree; nor does the supremacy clause recognize any distinction between laws of a State which must yield and those which need not yield to a conflicting exercise by Congress of its delegated powers.

The idea of a limited core of *absolutely* and *exclusively* reserved powers of the States not subject to the principle of national supremacy arose, as we saw, in the first instance chiefly out of the apprehensions of slavery. Even so, it never received the sanction of the Court till after the Civil War and then in a connection to which it was not relevant, namely, in assertion of the right of the *people of a State* to maintain a republican form of government along conventional American lines without interference from the National Government. The case referred to, *Collector v. Day*, represented the Court's revulsion from the contemporary Reconstruction legislation. It and derivative cases constitute a category apart.

The revival within recent decades of the notion that there are certain powers which are *exclusively* reserved to the States and in deference to their *possession* of which, therefore, the delegated powers of the United States must be defined, was the direct product of *laissez faire*-ism, and is still its instrument. Its practical purport is to claim for the States the exclusive power to govern production in most of its phases, and *especially as regards the relationship of employer and employee*. Certain accidental circumstances, however, aided this development. One was the appearance in 1899 of Tucker's work on the Constitution, in which the old Virginia States Rights theory of the Union as a mere congeries of "sovereign States" was pulled out of the grave and set up as an object of worship; and secondly, the accession of Justice White, a former Confederate soldier, to the bench.

Yet with all these favoring circumstances, Proposition IV has not fared well with the Court. In the field of the war power, in the field of treaty making, in the field of foreign commerce, States Rights have received scanty consideration in recent years,[1] while even in the field of interstate commercial regulation the attitude of the Court has been, as we have noted, shot through with inconsistency. Such decisions and accompanying opinions for the Court as those in the Lottery Case, the Hoke Case, the Minnesota Rate Cases, the Shreve-

---

[1] "In war we are one people. In making peace we are one people. In all commercial regulations, we are one and the same people." Chief Justice Marshall, in *Cohens v. Virginia*, Wheat. 264, 413. For the treaty-making power, see *Missouri v. Holland*, 252 U.S. 416 (1920); cf. *Prevost v. Greneaux*, 19 How. 1 (1856), where it is inferred that the treaty power is limited by the reserved powers of the States. For foreign commerce, see *University of Illinois v. United States*, 289 U.S. 48 (1933).

port Case cannot possibly be reconciled with acceptance of Proposition IV. Yet, as recent cases attest, Proposition V expresses what has today become a vital principle of constitutional law and theory. The corollary blooms and burgeons with little support from the doctrine from which it stems!

As was pointed out in Chapter 1, Marshall described Congress's power to regulate commerce among the States as "sovereign," "plenary," "complete in itself," and as "vested in Congress as absolutely as it would be in a single government" subject to the same express limitations as the National Government is. From this it necessarily follows that in judging the occasions for the exercise of this power and the ends to be forwarded by it, Congress is the sole judge, subject only to its political responsibility. Nor does Marshall leave this fact to inference. He likens Congress's discretion in the exercise of its power to regulate commerce among the States to its similarly unlimited discretion in declaring war.

What is more, Marshall in this respect but voiced the point of view of the period. Governmental powers were *sovereign* powers,[2] and the ends to be served by them, the motives inducing their exercise, could not furnish a

[2] Madison objected to Marshall's doctrine that they treated the powers of the General Government as "sovereign powers." *Writings* (Hunt, Ed.), VIII, 447-53. At other times, of course, he spoke of "sovereignty" being divided between the States and the United States.

constitutional limitation upon them that was susceptible of judicial application. This was so even as regards the taxing power, although that was capable of easy definition as the power to raise revenue. Indeed as late as 1904 we find Chief Justice White, ardent crusader that he was for dual federalism, asserting that, "The decisions of this Court from the beginning lend no support whatever to the assumption that the judiciary may restrain the exercise of lawful power on the assumption that a wrongful purpose or motive has caused that power to be exerted," and that the contrary proposition, "if sustained, would destroy all distinction between the powers of the respective departments of the government, would put an end to that confidence and respect for each other which it was the purpose of the Constitution to uphold, and would thus be full of danger to the permanence of our institutions."[3]

In 1922, nevertheless, in the Child Labor Tax Case this dangerous proposition *was* accepted by the Court as against the taxing power, and in the recent A. A. A. Case it was accepted as against the spending power. Furthermore, in the latter case the Court committed itself logically to the proposition that if an end can be served by the States on a *local* scale, the same end cannot be served by the National Government on a *broader* scale, thereby reviv-

[3] Pp. 230-1, *supra*.

ing Proposition IV in a new and exaggerated form.

And so we find ourselves confronted with the paradox that, with the country an economic and industrial unit, the prevailing trends of constitutional interpretation envisage it, so far as governmental regulation of business is involved, as *a confederation*. Indeed, the strictly legal situation is considerably more aggravated than this, for by invoking the right of the States to manage their "internal concerns" against national power one day and "national solidarity" against State power another, the Court has created for business a realm of *no-government* of generous dimensions;[4] and this realm it has further expanded at the expense of both governments by its theory of "due process of law" as *reasonable* law—in other words, law which *it* deems reasonable—and by its theory of "liberty" as signifying primarily the insulation of the employer-employee relationship from governmental regulation of any sort.[5] To the picture which past decisions have sometimes painted of a federal system "in which the national authority is maintained in full scope without

[4] See the present writer's "The Schechter Case—Landmark, or What?" in 13 *N.Y. Univ. L. Q. R.* (January 1936), 188-9, for a comparison between *Baldwin v. Seelig*, 294 U.S. 511 (decided March 4, 1935) and *Schechter Poultry Corp. v. United States*, 295 U.S. 495 (decided May 27, 1935).

[5] See e.g. the New York Minimum Wage Case, decided May 25th of the current term by a five-to-four Court.

unnecessary loss of local efficiency,"[6] recent decisions give the lie direct.

Interesting, nevertheless, as this aspect of the matter is theoretically, there is another of no less importance practically. This consists in the fact that on account of the competition among them in the interstate market, the States are unable in fact to exercise even the powers which in theory they still enjoy over business. In other words, if there is to be governmental regulation of business at all, it must be by the National Government. And not only is this the essential condition of *effectiveness*, it is also the essential condition of *public advantage*. The problem must be handled as a whole, and hence by the government which can so handle it. "In such matters there can be no divided empire."[7]

But this is exactly what recent decisions forbid. How, then, are they to be overcome? In what direction are we to look for the required remedy? While a constitutional amendment or amendments delegating further powers to the National Government is frequently suggested, certain objections at once occur. Why add to powers which, if properly construed, may be sufficient; and how can we

[6] Justice Hughes, in 230 U.S. 353, at 402.

[7] Quoted by the Chief Justice from *Green Bay Canal Co. v. Patten*, 172 U.S. 58, 80, in his opinion in *Ashwander v. T. V. A.*, decided February 17th of the current term. The "matters" referred to were improvement of navigation and the development of water power in navigable streams.

judge whether they *are* sufficient until they are properly construed? And of what avail would it be to subject new powers to the same process of construction as that which is demonstrably responsible for at least much of the gap needed to be filled? How long would the gap stay filled?[8]

Nor are such objections lessened when we turn to the Court's contemporary work in other fields than that of the substantive powers of Congress. We thereby learn that the Court has not one but many lethal weapons against legislation which, for any reason, it may regard unsympathetically. The Court can invalidate a statutory provision without challenging Congress's power to enact it, by asserting, in the very face of Congress's declaration to the contrary, that the latter would not have enacted the provision except in conjunction with other provisions which the

[8] As the Hon. John Dickinson has put it: "There is one problem which amendment will not solve and will not eliminate and which will remain no matter what amendments to the Constitution should be adopted. I refer, of course, to the problem of interpretation. Amendments themselves will have to be interpreted by lawyers and by courts, and their meaning and effect, like the meaning and effect of the Constitution as it now stands, will be at the mercy of the interpreters. No amendment can prove effective to adapt a Constitution to the needs of government if it is interpreted and applied, like the provisions which it was intended to supplement or correct, on assumptions which refuse to recognize the need for evolution and growth and the fact that evolution and growth may properly take place within the framework of the Constitution itself. There is no substitute for wise and enlightened interpretation; without it, the possibility of amendment is but a barren hope." 8 *Am. L. School R.*, 484 (May 1936).

Court holds to be unconstitutional.[9] The
Court can make measures which it concedes
to be constitutional practically ineffective
by the requirements which it lays down for
their enforcement—by setting up an incoher-
ent and ill-defined theory of the delegation of
legislative power;[10] by subjecting administrative findings of fact to a type of judicial review which has resulted in administrative
orders, finally held to be constitutional, being
suspended from twelve to fifteen years;[11] by
allowing private immunity a scope which gives
"immunity to guilt," encourages "falsehood
and evasion," and invites "the cunning and
unscrupulous to gamble with detection," thus
making "the statute and its sanctions . . .
the sport of knaves."[12] Finally—though further specifications might be adduced—mention must be made of the Court's virtual destruction of Section 3,224 of the Revised
Statutes, which forbids suits "for the purpose
of restraining the assessment or collection of
any tax." The gradual strangulation of this
provision in recent years makes a most extra-

[9] *Carter v. Carter Coal Co.*, decided May 15th of the current
term, by a Court splitting three ways.
[10] See especially Justice Cardozo's dissenting opinion in the
"Hot Oil" Cases, 293 U.S. 388 (January 7, 1935).
[11] See Justice Brandeis, speaking for himself and Justices Stone
and Cardozo, in *St. Joseph Stock Yards Co. v. United States*, decided April 27th of the current term.
[12] Justice Cardozo, speaking for himself and Justices Brandeis
and Stone, in *Jones v. Securities and Exchange Commission*,
decided April 6th of the current term.

ordinary chapter in the history of judicial power, the latest phase being the award by the Court of some $200,000,000 to people most of whom were probably not entitled to it.[13]

Now what, precisely, is the Amending Power to do in a situation like this? It might impose a curb on judicial review, and perhaps ought. Even so, we should still have the Court with us, and indeed could not get along without it. The problem would, therefore, still remain of gearing it into the rest of the National Government, of rendering it a cooperative part of that government. Is the Court to be deprived of its primary function of interpreting the law? If so, in what organ of government is this function to be vested? And should the Amending Power strike the "due process of law" clauses from the Constitution, and repeal the maxim against delegation of legislative power? Or should it leave these in their present distended form? Or should it formulate some midway version of them; and if so, in what terms?

The obvious fact is that such problems are much too intricate for the gross, fumbling hand of Amendment to deal with; and from this it follows that *we must still trust the Court, as we have so largely in the past, to correct its own errors*. Such trust has, moreover, been justified by the event, with the result that today the

[13] *Rickert Rice Mills v. Fontenot*, decided January 13th of the current term.

chief argument which could be urged against it, that based on the principle of *stare decisis*, has become a mere bugaboo. In the words of Justice Brandeis:

Stare decisis is not, like the rule of *res judicata*, a universal, inexorable command. "The rule of *stare decisis*, though one tending to consistency and uniformity of decision, is not inflexible. Whether it shall be followed or departed from is a question entirely within the discretion of the court, which is again called upon to consider a question once decided." *Hertz v. Woodman*, 218 U.S. 205, 212. *Stare decisis* is usually the wise policy, because in most matters it is more important that the applicable rule of law be settled than that it be settled right. Compare *National Bank v. Whitney*, 103 U.S. 99, 102. This is commonly true even where the error is a matter of serious concern, provided correction can be had by legislation. But in cases involving the Federal Constitution, where correction through legislative action is practically impossible, this Court has often over-ruled its earlier decisions. The Court bows to the lessons of experience and the force of better reasoning, recognizing that the process of trial and error, so fruitful in the physical sciences, is appropriate also in the judicial function. Compare *Brinkerhoff-Faris Trust & Sav. Co. v. Hill*, 281 U.S. 673, 681.[14]

[14] Dissenting opinion in *Burnet v. Coronado Oil and Gas Co.*, 285 U.S. 393, 405-9 and notes (1932). This was another five-to-four decision. "The doctrine of *stare decisis*, however appropriate and even necessary at times, has only a limited application in the field of constitutional law." Justice Stone, for himself and Justice Cardozo, in *St. Joseph Stock Yards Co. v. United States*, 80 Law Ed. Advance Opinions, 707. See also the same Justice's statement in the New York Minimum Wage Case, that he knew "of no rule or practice by which the arguments advanced in support of an application for *certiorari* restrict our choice between conflicting precedents in deciding a question of constitutional law. . . ."

And as the learned historian of the Constitution has phrased it:

However the Court may interpret the provisions of the Constitution, it is still the Constitution which is the law and not the decision of the Court.[15]

So, let the Court, abandoning the by-paths of contradictory doctrine and speculation regarding the relation of national and State power in which it has become involved in these latter days, retrace its steps to the highway of the clear-cut, straightforward, logically clean, historically authentic principles which are associated with the name of Marshall; more particularly, let it return again, as it has more than once in the past, to the reading which the great Chief Justice gave the commerce clause in *Gibbons v. Ogden*. Let it recognize that the power to regulate commerce among the States is the power to *govern* it, and hence the power to restrain it; that this power, like all other

ibid., 940. With this compare the following defense of the Court's decision in *Rickert Rice Mills v. Fontenot* (note 13, *supra*); "For so long as the Constitution of the United States endures in its present form, it must operate with the infallibility of the laws of nature. Sound and fecund growths will be fortified by its influences. Its impact will always strip the fruit from any governmental tree which is too defective to maintain its own integrity. The office of the Supreme Court is simply to elucidate the process." L. A. Janney in *New York Times*, May 5, 1935. Recurring to the subject of *stare decisis*, it should be noted that even in the private law field, a past decision must meet certain tests to be an eligible precedent. James Ram, *Science of Legal Judgment* (1871), 308 *ff*. It may be added that few of the Court's important constitutional holdings of recent date measure up very well to Mr. Ram's specifications.

[15] Charles Warren, *The Supreme Court in United States History*, III, 470.

powers of the National Government, is not limited by State power, but overrides any State power with which it comes into collision; that this power, moreover, is reposed by the *Constitution* in Congress and not in the Court, and so may be exercised for such objectives as Congress may select to promote, whether the Court likes them or not; that Congress has, in short, precisely the same power to prohibit any branch of commerce among the States as it has to prohibit any branch of foreign commerce, in furtherance of what it deems to be the general welfare.—All of which things Marshall said or logically implied. That the doctrines and theories manipulated by the Court in 1936 should deny Congress powers over interstate commerce which were recognized as belonging to it 112 years ago is a thing not only absurd in itself, but one which directly contradicts the notion of the Constitution as "a vehicle of national life."[16]

Closing his brilliant argument before the Court in *Carter v. Carter Coal Co.* a few weeks

[16] "The Supreme Court has declared the Federal Government has no power to control production nor any way to affect farm prices on the farm. That, it is declared, is a matter with which the States alone may deal. But five corporations, in no wise hindered by State lines, may, and do, control production and affect farm prices by fixing prices on the implements without which production cannot go forward. What the government may not do affirmatively, or negatively, may not do for want of power, private corporations are permitted to do regardless of States lines or State rights." Radio address of the Hon. W. E. Borah, May 12, 1936; *Cong. Record*, May 29, 1936, p. 8567.

since, Assistant Attorney General Dickinson said: "The issues are momentous. . . . The issue of Federal power is here at stake—whether there lurk within the interstices of the Constitution crevices through which Federal power may have sifted away."[17] In the six Propositions herein reviewed we see some of the crevices which Mr. Dickinson must have had in mind. That it is the power and duty of the Court to stop these, is the argument of this book.[18]

[17] The printed version (see pp. 249-50) is somewhat different.

[18] The case of *Whitefield v. Ohio*, mentioned on p. 170, *supra*, may be indicative that the Court is already beginning to stop some of the crevices just referred to—even while creating bigger ones! Should Congress pass a Child Labor Act after the model of the act sustained in the Whitefield Case, it is difficult to see how even the present Court could overthrow it.

TABLE OF CASES MENTIONED
IN TEXT

INDEX TO PERSONS QUOTED